This book is a work of non-fiction based on the life, experiences, and recollections of the author and four other survivors of stalking and abuse.

In some cases, the names of people have been changed to protect the privacy of others.

Voices Against Violence

Survivors Share Their Stories of Stalking and Abuse

Melissa Stockdale

Michael Terence
Publishing

Dedicated to anyone who has experienced or is currently experiencing stalking or domestic abuse.

Contents

Preface

I wrote the book: **'Voices Against Violence: Survivors Share Their Stories of Stalking and Abuse'** after fleeing from a violent and abusive partner. I survived his brutal attack and his attempt to strangle me, and I managed to escape. However, I then suffered further trauma as I was relentlessly stalked by him after this. I was living each day in constant fear of him finding me and harming me. During this anxious time, I struggled to find the mental strength and the physical energy that I really needed to be able to successfully manage the arduous task of interacting with the police and lawyers to gain the necessary protection and justice that I deserved.

I hope that after reading this book, those who find themselves trapped in an abusive and controlling relationship will gain more knowledge, feel more enlightened and informed, and therefore be better prepared for the process required to seek the appropriate help. The information provided within my book will also enable survivors to manage the challenging tasks ahead of them more effectively.

I was fortunate to have been wisely advised by my doctor and a clinical psychologist who cared for me immediately after being violently attacked, to diligently record the details of all the abuse directed towards me, no matter how seemingly insignificant. They stressed to me how vitally important it was to include times, dates and locations, along with the names and contact information of any witnesses. Through this simple act of daily record keeping, I amassed an extensive timeline that I was able to share with the police, and this evidence helped considerably to bring my perpetrator successfully to court. In addition, keeping a personal regular written account of these events served as a therapeutic tool. It helped me to recognise the pattern of abuse, and in doing so, it also gave me the mental strength to be able to accept what was happening to me.

When reading the four candid accounts of each of the victims' personal experiences of abuse and stalking within each chapter of this book, you may identify with similarities of certain events or behaviours within your own situation. If this is the case, **'Voices Against Violence: Survivors Share Their Stories of Stalking and Abuse'** provides the details of various relevant charities and specialist agencies where you will be able to find the necessary free help and the appropriate support to aid your disentanglement from an abusive relationship.

There are example forms within this book, which can be used to record the vital information that you may wish to present to the police. Once completed, these forms will assist in the building of a strong case against the perpetrator; hopefully secure justice and help to acquire the appropriate legal protection for your future.

For anyone who is caught up in an intimate relationship that they have genuine concerns about, I would implore them to make an application via the **Domestic Violence Disclosure Scheme (DVDS)** also known as **'Clare's Law'** *https://clares-law.com/*. I made my application to discover the facts about my partner's criminal past. Having this important information disclosed to me was empowering, and it also enabled me to make informed decisions about my future. In addition, the disclosure assisted the Judge during the legal process and helped to secure an appropriate restraining order. It also provided invaluable information for the court to be able to make the correct decisions concerning additional protection being put in place for my future safety.

Under **'Clare's Law'** you can apply for information about your current or ex-partner because you feel that you are at risk, or you are worried that they may have a history of abuse. Equally, a friend or a relative may also request information on your behalf if they have concerns that you may be at risk.

Dr Katerina Hadjimatheou has extensively researched the value to victims and survivors who have made applications to **'Clare's Law'**. She says:

'If you are in an abusive relationship, it can be important to know that you are not the only one and that the abuse is not your fault. If someone has a history of violence or control with different partners it means your abuse is unlikely to stop, whatever you do. Information can help you to build confidence, strength and faith in your own judgement and to make informed decisions about your own safety.' (Hadjimatheou, Dr. K, 10th October 2023).

'And once the storm is over, you won't remember how you made it through, how you managed to survive. You won't ever be sure, whether the storm is really over. But one thing is certain. When you come out of the storm, you won't be the same person who walked in. That's what this storm's all about'.

Haruki Murakami
(Kafka on the Shore, 2005)

Introduction

All the victims/survivors who kindly volunteered to contribute their personal stories to my book did so willingly in the hope that the process of doing so would be therapeutic and beneficial for their own recovery. In addition, they sincerely hope that their voices will provide helpful insight for others who may be currently experiencing or have experienced the trauma of stalking, violent attacks, and/or abusive relationships.

Each of the stories in this book involves a woman who has been abused by a man. However, it is important to recognise that there are also cases reported where stalking and abuse have occurred within same-sex relationships where males or females are the victims. Smaller numbers of men are stalked and psychologically abused by women, although the exact figures are hard to determine as men are often less inclined to report such incidents to the police possibly through fear of being ridiculed.

Having personally suffered and struggled through the harrowing experience of psychological domestic abuse, non-fatal strangulation, violence and stalking from 2019 to 2022, I consider myself to be a 'survivor'. However, I do recognise that many others who have experienced similar crimes will perceive their position very differently, and indeed, they may not wish to be labelled in any way at all. Therefore, the terms 'victims' and 'survivors' will be used interchangeably throughout this book when relating events.

Personally, I found it completely disempowering to be labelled a 'victim' by members of the police and the court system.

It takes tremendous strength and bravery for victims/survivors to initially come forward to report their intimate experience of domestic abuse, sexual abuse, violence, or stalking. However, it is often the unfolding investigative process that follows the initial reporting of a crime, which can be even more distressing and intrusive for the victim. Therefore, I would like to express my deepest gratitude to each person who kindly contributed their experiences for this book. I thank them for having the confidence to agree to share their stories for this publication, and for freely giving up their time and energy to relate their life-changing events with such complete honesty and openness.

For the sake of humanising each person, I have entitled each chapter with the name of the person to whom it relates. For anonymity and at personal request by the contributors, some of these names have been changed, and the exact places where their crimes took place have been omitted. This is to protect their identities, preserve their privacy, to prevent further intrusion by unknown parties, and obviously to continue to keep each person safe from their known perpetrators.

I do recognise that recalling these traumatic events may have been challenging and upsetting for them, and the process could have possibly caused further emotional turmoil. During each interview, there was often a mixture of laughter and tears. However, it is interesting to note that most of the participants expressed to me that being able to relay their complete story in a non-judgemental arena was empowering for them. They informed me that after being able to recount their full story, they felt less burdened, and in addition, they found the process of relating their personal events to someone else who had suffered similar experiences assisted them in their psychological recovery.

Every participant told me that the traumatic process of having to report the crime to the police had noticeably affected them. The terminology that is regularly used by professionals is often difficult for victims to comprehend, and there is a presumption by police officers that all people who report their crimes will be able to automatically understand the terminology and the specific use of certain acronyms that they commonly use. As a traumatized victim who is appealing for help, it can feel like they are entering an alien world where there is a completely different language being spoken.

Each victim/survivor explained to me that they had struggled in some form whilst navigating their way through the long, arduous, and mentally demanding task of presenting their evidence and that they found it hard having to explain and repeat the facts of their individual case in such a prescriptive and concise way. They did, however, recognise that it was necessary for them to engage in the appropriate legal manner which is required if they wished to seek justice.

Sadly, it is often the case that the victims' voices and their feelings are not fully understood or considered during the reporting of the crime. Their voices may not be fully heard while preparing evidence, or even indeed during the court proceedings that may follow. The arduous and debilitating process of preparing for trial can initiate and expose a range of powerful emotions ranging from complete breakdown and devastation, where victims may decide to give up on their case and withdraw their charges, to those who feel completely overwhelmed and suicidal.

Some victims feel so traumatised, vulnerable, and insignificant, that they may not have the mental capacity to fully engage in the process of promoting their own fight for justice. In contrast to this, other victims may exhibit a more extreme reactive behaviour of anger and rage and will relish having their day in court.

One survivor, Anne, expressed to me that she felt extremely let down when her **'Personal Impact Statement'**, which she had painstakingly taken weeks to write was completely ignored and therefore was not read out aloud during the court proceedings as she had hoped and expected it would be. In addition, Anne was incensed that her daughter's killer showed zero remorse for his actions. Anne, who is classified as a *'secondary victim'* being the mother of the victim, was equally devastated when the perpetrator was only eventually sentenced to 16 years in prison for killing her daughter.

Anne decided that the only way to have her voice fully heard would be to approach her local newspaper to request that they print her personal story so she could relay her heartfelt comments and publicly express how the murder of her daughter, Rebecca, had destroyed her life. Talking about the perpetrator, Anne's words were reported in the newspaper: *"If he is released in 16 or 17 years, he will come out my age, and I have a life sentence for the rest of my life"* (Nuttall, D, 2007, updated 2021).

There have been other similar cases where a survivor's anger has led them to have no alternative but to arrange to meet with the press to have their words printed in the public arena. For example, Sam Taylor poignantly told the

Guardian newspaper: *"I have to speak out. That's what keeps me sane"* (Day, 2013, p 20). I have huge admiration for the bravery of such individuals.

The tragic stories included in this book have been written down using the survivor's own words following face-to-face taped interviews. I hope that my additional text in each chapter provides an accurate interpretation of their personal events, demonstrates the immense suffering that they have been through and illustrates the never-ending impact on their lives. I apologise to those who may feel that the following transcripts of these taped interviews do not provide a full enough description of their experiences.

All the survivors who have shared their stories have suffered some form of PTSD (Post Traumatic Stress Disorder), and their lives have been significantly altered in the aftermath of the violation caused by their perpetrators. It has been repeatedly documented how the effects of experiencing stalking and domestic abuse will often cause lifelong consequences, leaving physical and mental health issues which linger on well after the violence has ended. (Fergusson, Horwood & Ridder, 2005; Korkodeilou, 2020; Mechanic, Weaver & Resick, 2008).

Regarding the violent acts that I personally endured, I sought help from my local police, and they quickly signposted me to the offices of **'Lighthouse Women's Aid'**. Without the immediate support from this charitable organisation, I am not sure how I would have navigated my way through the fear and emotional turmoil that I was suffering. I would like to thank the staff at **'Lighthouse Women's Aid'** who genuinely listened to my story, believed me, and demonstrated to me that they understood my situation, and truly cared.

Writing poetry provided an outlet for the outpouring of intense emotions that were consuming me during the most frightening and stressful times of being relentlessly harassed and stalked by the man who violently attacked me. It was a soothing relief to be able to express my feelings out loud, write them down, read them back, and be able to have a simple way of sharing my deepest intimate thoughts with others.

I have included several of my poems in this publication in the hope of inspiring others who may be suffering abuse. Perhaps they may also try to write poems, stories, or songs as a therapeutic tool for expressing their hurt and inner frustrations. Other survivors of violent crimes have reported to me that they have noticed a positive restoration of their mental health by engaging in other creative activities such as: outdoor exercise, yoga, meditation, drama, dance, writing journals, drawing, and painting.

On a personal note, I was one of the fortunate survivors who was also able to access regular sessions with an eminent psychotherapist. His kindness and his professional expertise in this area helped considerably in navigating my way through the trauma, darkness, and extreme fear that I was feeling. He has kindly provided the foreword for this publication.

I hope that this book will enable those who have contributed their stories to feel a certain relief now that they have openly shared their life-changing experiences. Their detailed and frank accounts will also allow the reader to gain a real insight into the psychological harm, and the devastating, lasting emotional impact that is caused by being a victim of stalking and/or abuse. Hopefully, these stories will also encourage those people who may feel trapped in similar dangerous situations to be able to make that brave first step towards seeking help.

Allowing people to tell their stories really does matter as the process helps them to repair and heal their wounds, and therefore restores their dignity. Being listened to and believed assists them in overcoming the violation they have suffered. As Jenny Korkodeilou revealed in her recent book: **'Victims of Stalking – Case Studies in Invisible Harms'** - *'Survivors of stalking can more easily regain their voices, agency, power and strength when they have their often-uncomfortable truths heard'*. (Korkodeilou, 2020, p126).

If you are experiencing stalking or abuse, please seek help and support, and report the crime to police. There is a list of some of the relevant agencies and organisations that can offer advice and assistance in the final pages of this book.

'Each person feels pain in his own way,
each has his own scars.'

Haruki Murakami
(Kafka on the Shore, 2005)

No Words

There are no words that can explain,
The way I feel, the hurt, the pain.
The injuries are deep inside,
They come and go, just like the tide.

A wave arrives and crashes down,
Suffocating with its deadly sound.
My voice within is trying to shout,
But no words will come and venture out.

How can these feelings stay within?
And hurt so much inside my skin.
Let me out! I hear them say,
My dignity just blocks the way.

The time will come when I will see
The importance of just being me.
To face the negative thoughts at last,
Look forward and release the past.

Melissa Stockdale
(2020)

Foreword

by Sn Emrys D.Hyp, HG.Dip.P, MA (HG. Psych),
FHOCC, MAEPH, MHGI, METSI.Suffolk,
Ostara 2023

Emrys is a fully qualified, university-educated registered psychotherapist in private practice with 45 years of pastoral and clinical experience. His speciality areas include but are not limited to sub-threshold ASC (Autistic Spectrum Condition); PTSD (Post-Traumatic Stress Disorder); ACEs (Adverse Childhood Experiences), Coercive Relationships; and Chronic-Pain Resolution. He also works in general psychotherapeutic practice with children and adults with an extensive range of morbidities from para-suicide to phobias.

When I was asked to write the foreword for this book, I thought I'd do some research into my past case histories. When I averaged out the relevant cases I was shocked to discover that almost every week for the past forty-five years, I've found myself face-to-face in my clinic with at least one woman whose life was a living nightmare because of her abusive/stalking partner. One of these women was the author of this book.

Melissa's own story spans years. Her perpetrator followed her across continents and his behaviour could make him the poster-boy for those of his ilk: attempting to strangle her, theft, deceit, threats, stalking at its creepiest level, lying to her friends, lying to the police and the courts, and lying and manipulating anybody else who got in his way, using people who could be useful to him, discarding them, then, of course, claiming to be the victim.

My case-notes are full of this kind of behaviour; women dangled over cliff edges, strangled with telephone cords; theft and fraud - sometimes to the tune of millions, but more usually of less monetary magnitude but of priceless emotional value, chief amongst which is the theft of a person's sense of self-worth; relentless gas-lighting to a point where many victims actually come to believe that they're mad; days and nights filled with dread; too scared to use or answer the phone; children being weaponised; isolation from friends and family; scared to go out in case the perpetrator is there, lurking, waiting; unable to trust anyone because the perpetrator has done such a good job on manipulating everybody the victim knows. The list goes on and on.

Maybe you see yourself in this list, maybe you know someone who's confided in you, or hinted that they are experiencing these things. If so, you need to read the stories of the courageous women in this book. You'll find that they are survivors, not victims, their stories; real stories from real women will give you hope; and then you need to act upon Melissa's clear and concise guidance, which will set you on the path to freedom and peace.

In many respects, her story is very typical of the women (and occasionally men) that I see: far removed from the archetypical images that many people unfamiliar with the reality of controlling, traumatising behaviour think. Such people often assume those on the receiving end of such treatment must be stupid or that there's 'something wrong with them' and while that may be true in a minority of cases (because years of trauma can switch the thinking-brain off to some degree) my direct experience is quite the opposite.

Coercive behaviour and stalking know no societal or intellectual boundaries. I've seen it happen to dinner-ladies, movie stars, people living on benefits, medical practitioners, multi-millionaires, sex-workers, politicians, lesbian couples and shop workers. It cuts across age, sex, colour, caste, and creed.

Recent years have seen a seismic shift in the response to the crime of coercive control. Thanks to the inexorable demand for justice by a small army of fearless, resolute women and a relatively tiny number of their champions in the male form, parliament finally pushed through **Section 76 of the Serious Crime Act 2015** making it a serious criminal offence to stalk, harass, coerce, control, and of course to visit upon or threaten violence physically or mentally, toward an intimate or family-relationship partner. It is updated regularly.

So, can we assume that all is well now? Have perpetrators stopped perpetrating? Of course not! Swathes of my case history notes bear witness to the veracity of the stories in this book: difficulty providing enough, or the correct forms of evidence; the police understaffed thanks to successive cuts to their service; a reprehensible lack of specially trained or even just understanding/ compassionate officers; a ridiculously long backlog of court dates (partly due to the Covid pandemic, partly because of systemic cuts to the legal system), and a shameful shortage of safe refuges, etcetera.

I know a lot of victims simply give up hope of ever moving on as they feel the system is against them; some of course are still too afraid or have been manipulated to believe that there is no hope and therefore resign themselves to continue life with the perpetrator as their only option. That is why Melissa's book is so important. It pulls no punches regarding the reality of the situation many victims face when seeking to escape from and eventually, hopefully, prosecute the perpetrators for all the crimes committed against them.

Melissa's book is a beacon, no, a laser beam that shines bright in the midst of this darkness and directs you out of it. She and the women who have contributed to it have survived their ordeals and have managed to come out fighting. She lays out how to recognise coercive/stalking behaviour when it's happening, what to do about it, where to find help and support, what evidence you need to gather and how to get it. And she does so in a way that is simple, to the point, and, as she can attest from her own experience: works.

I have a mantra for female victims of male abusive partners: *'If he hits you once, whether physically or mentally, leave and don't look back; because if you don't, you've given him carte blanche to do it again. And he will: again, and again, and again and again and again.'*

It is my hope that if you are in such a relationship, then reading **'Voices Against Violence: Survivors Share their Stories of Stalking and Abuse'** will help you. It will give you hope, and guide you to the resources to be able to free yourself. If you are not in such a relationship, then I hope that the stories in the book will enrage you to the point where you get up, join us, and do something to help those who *are* suffering in this way.

The Effects of Abuse

I was fearless – Now I am fearful
I was happy – Now I am sad
I was strong – Now I am weak
I was positive – Now I am negative
I was energetic – Now I am tired
I was resilient – Now I am vulnerable
I was sociable – Now I am reclusive
I was working – Now I am unemployed
I was big – Now I am small
I was complete – Now I am broken
I was healthy – Now I am unhealthy
My hair was shiny – Now it's dull
My skin was clear – Now it's blemished
My eyes were bright – Now they are sore
My mind was lucid – Now it's muddled
I was full of hope – Now I am full of dread

I fear this man who wants me dead.

Melissa Stockdale
(2020)

19

1

LOUISE

'Life is a Pantomime'

(Interviewed March 2022)

Louise who was groomed and gang-raped when she was seventeen years old has since been a victim of domestic abuse multiple times at the hands of several different men. She has endured over eighteen years of abuse.

'His eyes would glaze over and a different person would beam out of his eyes. It was scary.'

I think the help you get depends on where you live. It is a bit of a postcode lottery. If the abuse you are experiencing takes place across different counties, then it means that two different police forces will often be involved, and this sometimes causes problems with the matter reaching court or achieving justice. Often cases get dropped, and the perpetrators make up excuses and they get away with their crimes.

What frustrates me the most is that often I think the police can see what is happening, and they try to help, but the CPS (Crown Prosecution Service), seems to be more reluctant to persist with the charges. It seems to me, that there are other cases that the police deem to be more important to deal with and therefore things need to escalate to a very dangerous stage with domestic abuse before they will decide to do anything about it. It is crazy.

Abusers terrorise people. They seem to enjoy intimidating others, and they love the attention they get. They continue with what they are doing as they know that they will get away with it. They also enjoy manipulating the police, and some will even falsely accuse a woman of doing things so that the police will turn up on the woman's doorstep to question them. The perpetrators do this deliberately as they know it will affect their victim, and that it will cause them considerable embarrassment, anxiety and stress. This makes them feel powerful and in control. It is like they are getting the police to do their dirty work for them.

I received a lot of help from Women's Aid. Just realising that it wasn't just me who was experiencing all this stuff, really helped me. The staff at Woman's Aid validated my thoughts and my feelings, and they took away some of the shame that I was feeling. Knowing that there is now a big push in the UK to recognise that domestic abuse is a serious crime, I realise that I can no longer allow myself to be minimised, or allow people to use **'gaslighting' (1)** techniques on me anymore.

I have suffered abuse from several different men in my lifetime. I have tried to move away from the cycle of this happening to me. I am trying to stop myself from being so vulnerable, and trying to stop allowing these men from taking advantage of me. I found that men I would meet would try to use my own abusive past against me to make me feel weak, and make me believe that the problems are my fault. They made me feel like I am the one to blame and that I deserve it. This fact makes it even less likely for me to have the confidence to be able to report future abusive behaviour to the police.

My family and friends have been truly supportive, although, I have lost a few friends along the way who became *'flying monkeys'* **(2)**, as I like to call them (laughs). Yes, I heard it said at a women's support group, that these people are called *'flying monkeys'* as they have been deliberately turned against me by the things that my partner may have said to them, and then they have spread the words they hear to others. It really explains the term *'flying monkeys'* well.

I now have a good job and I am doing well. I did some **EMDR therapy** (Eye Movement Desensitisation and Reprocessing) **(3)**, which saved my life. EMDR therapy really helped with the PTSD (Post Traumatic Stress Disorder). It was hard to do the therapy, but it was worth it. I am a single mum with two children and I run my own home, and I am doing a job that I really love. I am in complete control of my life now, and I stand up to bullies in every area of my life. I am ready to show others that your life is not ruined by what you have experienced. It changes you, yes, but I now know that I have a super power for sniffing out narcissists! My advice is to keep those eyes wide open, as narcissists thrive on reactions. So, starve them! We should not have to live with people like that. We need to get stronger and more resilient and stand up to them.

I went through a chain reaction in my relationships of being vulnerable and falling into the hands of the next man just because they were trying so hard to be kind and nice to me. One of them even sent me some money into my bank account, just to try to send me a message (laughs). It does make me laugh sometimes to realise how pathetic they can really be. Did they all go to the same college to learn this behaviour together? They all use the same similar controlling tactics. I learnt a lot about this from the staff at Women's Aid and from comparing stories with others at support groups. For example, like the common tactic of men asking for a DNA test to prove that the children you have together are his. They seem to try to find any way that they possibly can to cause us deliberate obstruction, harm and distress.

They will also deliberately try to incite fear. For example, my ex, when we broke up as he was leaving the house he pointed to my window locks on the way out, and he said to me: *"I think you need to change those as someone could easily get in here."* He was just saying this to make me think about the possibility of him coming back and breaking in.

It annoys me that my daughter is so affected by the abuse that I have endured. I have experienced so much abuse. I can only talk about it now as I have had therapy for a few years. Now I have got boundaries set in place.

My first experience happened when I was 14 years old, and I am 37 years old now.

My first boyfriend was very full-on, and he did a lot of what they call **'love bombing' (4)** to me. I was only 14 when I first met him and I was vulnerable, and I had very little self-confidence and no boundaries in place. I am a very empathetic person and I always see the best in people. I have snippets of memories from that time (pause). I remember that I tried to split up with him, but then he would come up to the bay window of my home and he would knock on my window in the middle of the night and stuff. I remember running through into my mum's bedroom, as I was so scared. I would jump into bed with her, but I would not tell her why. I was absolutely terrified that my boyfriend would wake up my mum.

He was also violent towards me. I managed to end this abusive relationship eventually, but I have never forgotten that fear of wondering if, and when he would turn up again, and then the fear of what he might do to me next. I would think: *'What will he do if he gets to me?'* I was so worried that I would get in trouble from my mum. I was with him for a year or so. He talked me into having sex with him and I ended up pregnant. It was awful as I was only 15 years old and my mum was mad with me. I was told to have an abortion, but I was confused, and I did not know what to do.

One night, my boyfriend came round to my house. He had been drinking, and my mum was out working. My mum was trying to hold down three jobs to look after us and she was working at the pub that night. I tried to tell him to leave, but he began arguing with me and he punched me hard in my tummy. I remember thinking then that I can't have this baby with this person. So, I went to have the abortion. Then afterwards, I felt this massive shame for having the abortion. Obviously, this did not help with my self-esteem issues, and everything else. Back in those days, issues like this were swept under the carpet, and we were told not to let anyone know. There was no mental health support offered then, not like you would get these days. I had no one to talk to.

I remember, my boyfriend turned up at the hospital after the abortion with a bar of chocolate and he gave it to me, and then he left. I looked at it and I just thought:

'What is that?' (Laughs) *'It was ridiculous – a bar of chocolate? Oh yeah great!'* (Laughs) *'That makes everything better!'*

People at my school found out about the abortion and there was a lot of bullying at school, so it was not a good place for me to be. I remember that I then started drinking, and I began to get into more trouble. I did ok at school, so I went on to college, as I really wanted to be an accountant. I made friends with a man at college who seemed nice. He seemed to always be there for me and he would pick me up and take me places. He would say to me, *"I will always listen to you. I am there for you."* I did not realise it at the time, but he was in fact grooming me. He would supply me with alcohol, as he knew that I was struggling with my own addiction to alcohol. One night he spiked my drink and he took me to a house where there was a group of Asian men who all took turns to rape me. I did not tell anyone about it at the time (pause). I think I only told one person about this then, but now other people know. When I look back, I think that I chose not to tell anyone as I was so ashamed, and I thought that they would think I was a 'slag' which is a common term used towards women with the intention to shame women.

The memory of the rape is very blurry (pause). I remember going in and out of consciousness at the time, (pause), and I remember lots of people. Yeah… (Long pause). I didn't feel that I could go home and talk to my mum about this. I then began to go off the rails. I left home and I went to live with my dad. He's not that great, so that didn't work. He just goes to the pub and drinks. I remember asking him if I could go and live with him, but he was hesitant, and he said: *"Oh, I don't know."*

I felt that nobody loved me and that I was not worth anything. There was no other place to find support, and I was trying to put a mask on the whole time. I began to self-harm. I have huge scars on my arm here (points to her arm) from self-harming. I now have a tattoo over them. Lady Gaga designed this tattoo. It is a survivor tattoo, called a 'fire rose unity survivor' and it was specially designed for people who have survived sexual abuse. Lots of people have got this tattoo, and it is a sort of mark for the community for people who have survived. Not everyone knows what it means.

It used to be an on-going joke with my family that I am a weirdo magnet. It is true, weirdoes always seem to be attracted to me and want to talk to me, and they latch on. I can't seem to get rid of them. I took my car in for a service in a garage once when my daughter was very young, and when I dropped the car off there, the mechanic began talking to me. He had my phone number so that he could contact me when the car was ready, and after I collected my car, he began to persistently call me to ask me out. I said no, but he kept pestering and pestering me, and I had to keep telling him to leave me alone.

I began taking recreational drugs at the weekends. I think I did this just to try and get away from things, like the hurt and pain and cutting myself, etc. I studied hard, but I also partied hard too. Thankfully, I got my qualifications in the end.

I had a few more dodgy relationships along the way, but they did not really turn into anything. I had male friends who had been friends of mine for years, and then they would also try it on with me. As soon as I would turn them down, they would turn nasty. They would not like me turning them down, but they continued to persist. I would say to them clearly: *"No, that's a NO!"* (Laughs). I am not sure what is wrong with them. They just stay around pushing somebody, and they persist for so long. They think that they will get their way in the end maybe?

I did meet someone else when I was 19. Things moved fast, and we moved in together along with his young daughter. So, I became a step-mum at 19 years of age, and I was doing everything that I could for his daughter. He was very controlling. He built it up bit by bit. He would make negative comments about what I wore. Comments about men at work too. If I came home and told him about men at work, he would get angry. I quickly learnt not to come home and talk about work, or men at work because if I mentioned a man's name from work, like Sean, then he would make derogatory comments to me and say: *"Oh I bet you are shagging Sean."*

If I arrived home a few minutes late from work, I would start to get reprimanded by him. If I did join friends from work on the way home, I would dread what would happen to me when I got home. He got increasingly bad, and he would strangle me when I got in. He would pin me up and strangle me. His eyes would glaze over and a different person would beam out of his eyes. It was scary. That to me is the scariest thing in the world, and it has happened to me with other men. When I see those eyes, then I know that this is it. You do not know what is going to happen next. It is so unpredictable. It is a sign to watch out for. It is like walking on eggshells. It increases your anxiety and that fear within you. You just do not know what is going to happen next.

When I was younger, I could be very bolshie and I thought I could stick up for myself. I could hold my own and I could argue back, whereas now when somebody does that to me, I would get out of there. Mind you, you cannot always get out of there, as they lock you in the house and you cannot get out, so you do not know what to do and you must stand up for yourself. When it happens time and time again, you don't know what to do. But I stayed, because of the little girl.

His friends knew what he was like. They knew that he was unpredictable, but they never held him accountable. He would behave like this in front of our friends and kick off on one. Anyway, I remember once seeing my best friend, Thomas, in the bar, and I had not seen him for ages so I went to give him a big hug. When my partner saw this, he came flying across the bar at me shouting and screaming, and he punched Thomas.

One night though, I did ring the police after he had been strangling me, but it took a long time of suffering for me to eventually phone the police. He pinned me down on the bed with his knee and he had his knee on my neck. I managed to get away and I managed to call the police. He barricaded himself in the bedroom and the police forced their way in and they took him out. This is when I was around 20 or 21 years old.

The police took him away and I called my mum. Then I went to my mum's house, as his little girl was not there with us that night. She was staying with his mum. Later, the police came round to talk to me and they were absolutely disgusted with him. They turned to me and said: *"What do you want to do? Do you want to press charges?"* I just wanted it all to be over with and to go away. I did not want to have to explain myself, or go to court to face him. I just wanted to get my stuff out of that house and get away from him. That was all I wanted. But the police wanted to arrest him. The police were laughing, and saying that they had to extract small pieces of my nails from the scratches on his face where I had struggled to get away from him, and from where I was trying to protect myself (laughs). There was never any doubt from the police that this was in self-defence.

I do often wonder, that maybe, if I had been supported in a different way at that time, then I could have gone through with pushing the charges against him further, but I was so traumatised when it happened.

When I reported a case of abuse by another man a few years later, the support was very different and I was immediately given a list of agencies like **'Women's Aid'** and **'Victim Support'** that could help me. The agencies were always ringing me, and checking up on me. There was a time before this that they did not talk about mental health issues, but it is so different now, and more help is currently available.

I met my ex-husband when I was 22 years old; we were together for seven years and we had two children together. He seemed much nicer than the other guys, but I was still taking a few drugs at the time when we met. He was taking different drugs, and he encouraged me to take those too. Drugs like soft Ketamine and other recreational drugs. He was quite the boy next-door, and he seemed kind and nice with a soft-looking face. He was not a thug, and he had not been in trouble with the police before. He was not aggressive or violent, but it turned out that he was extremely manipulative, and it took me several years to see this.

I did not know anything about emotional abuse, or psychological manipulation then. He wasn't hitting me, and he wasn't kicking off when he was drunk. He was better, you know (pause). If we disagreed on anything, he would always go below the belt though, and he would say nasty comments to me. We would argue about whether we were having carrots for tea, Then, you know, he would say hurtful things like: *"Your dad does not love you. It's no wonder your dad wants nothing to do with you."* He knew how to really hurt me.

He knew that I did not have a very good relationship with my father, and he knew that this was probably one of the reasons why I did not have much self-love. I often used to think that I was not loveable and stuff. I don't want to blame my parents, but I think that the arguments and their divorce really did affect me. My sister and I were always caught in the middle and we used to think: *'Well what about us?'*

I would go off the rails and be naughty, and even now my parents accuse me of being a very difficult teenager. It was hard for me. When I reflect on it now, and I think: *Why was I behaving that way? Why was I doing that?* But no one was talking to me then. I can see that clearly now, but only because I have had therapy. I make sure now that I do not talk to my children about their dad in a negative way. I want them to have two happy family homes.

When we were engaged, my fiancé became increasingly manipulative and unsupportive, and it became even worse when I found out that I was pregnant. He stopped me from talking about the pregnancy for the first six months, as he said that he was not ready for it. Bless him! (Laughs). Yeah, everything was always about him. He was immature, and he did not want to talk about it, but somehow, I convinced myself that eventually, he would come round to it. It was an unexpected pregnancy, we were newly engaged, and we had just got a dog, so I began to make excuses for him, thinking that he was just immature.

We lived together and we both had good jobs. I said to him: *"Ok, well yes this pregnancy is a bit unexpected, but let's talk about it."* He told me that he wanted to travel, and that I was ruining his life, and that it was all my fault. I thought to myself, hang on, we both did that, it can't be all me (laughs).

I began to feel so lonely in the relationship. We persevered, and the relationship went up and down, and then we had the baby. When I brought her home though, he just shouted at the baby. In front of other people, he would make out that he was doing lots to help, and he would pretend that he was being very supportive, but when the people left, he became hard work. He complained constantly about the baby for keeping waking up, and for being hungry, and crying. I said to him; *"But it's a baby. It's what they do."* It is life-changing. His behaviour terrified me, as he would scream at the baby in her face as he was holding her. He complained to me that he couldn't cope, as he was too tired, etc. It was always about him.

When she was a few months old, I remember leaving him with her for the night and saying to him: *"Look you have got to get on with this, I need a break."* His excuse was that he was working, but he was also out at the pub every night or out rehearsing for plays and being on TV shows with his friends. Despite having a baby, he was still doing everything that he wanted to do, and even taking part in a pantomime!

He would be nasty and make cutting comments to me, and bring up sad things that had happened to me in the past. For example, he brought up about my friend, Thomas, who had been killed recently in an incident at work. He was killed on a crane. My partner made out that he was also really devastated and upset about it, but then he continued saying all these cruel things to me, and he did not support me, which brought on my depression. All of this happened at time where I was trying my best to bring up my daughter. He showed absolutely no care or concern for me at all (pause). My daughter saved my life in a way. We are so close now, and I don't know what I would do without her.

If I tried to make things better, he became worse. I decided to get some therapy, but then he made me feel such shame for seeking therapy, or for getting help from the health visitors. The health therapists were kind and helpful, but I still found it difficult to tell anyone about the rapes that had happened to me when I was younger. Now, I think that if I could have talked about the rapes to them then, I might have got better sooner. At this time, I was still in and out of self-harming, and my partner knew about that, so I knew that if I tried to end the relationship, he would use this against me. When eventually I did confide in him about the rapes, he would then use this new knowledge in our arguments. He would try to minimise the fact that I was raped. He knew that things would trigger me and upset me, and therefore, during arguments, he would always bring up about the rapes to deflect from what he had done.

We discussed about having another baby, but he would keep changing his mind about it. He would say: *"Ok, we can have another baby after we are married."* So, we got married and we had a wonderful wedding, but I remember thinking at the time: *Do I really want to do this?* I remember panicking, but then trying to convince myself that it was the right thing to do. We were both trying to make it better, and we both got on well with each other's friends, so it seemed that it would work, and from the outside, it looked like the right thing to do. However, when I thought about all the arguments that we had, I realised how manipulative he was. I knew how he would gaslight me, and accuse me of things. He did cheat on me once, but he was always telling me that I was the one who was paranoid and crazy. In my heart, I knew that it was wrong, but for some reason, I still went through with it.

A few months after we were married, I got pregnant again with our second child, but then I lost the baby at thirteen and a half weeks. I remember finding out that something was wrong when I had the twelve-week scan. In the hospital in front of other people, my husband made out to everyone there that he was this kind, supportive, and helpful man, but as soon as we got home and we were alone he was totally different, and he showed absolutely no concern for my feelings.

Friends came round one night to see us both when we came back from the hospital, but no one seemed to care about me losing my baby. They were just getting stoned and stuff, so I went to bed. When I woke up in the morning and went downstairs, I could see that they had left a real mess, and coffee had been spilt all over the carpet. I remember being on my hands and knees trying to clean up the stains on the carpet. I was feeling so devastated about the fact that I was losing my baby, and I was wondering why I was the one who was having to clean up their mess. It was so inconsiderate. I realised then, that my husband was not a supportive man. He did not support me when my best friend died, and he is not supporting me now. I really began to resent him.

When we lost the baby and I had to go into hospital, my other daughter, who was only three, also had to go into hospital. I was worrying about this, but believe it or not, my husband just sat around doing a crossword (laughs). At the time, my husband was taking part in a pantomime and he seemed more concerned about whether he would miss the opening night of the pantomime rather than caring for our daughter and me.

I was staying in the hospital caring for my 3-year-old daughter for four or five days and this was in the floor above the maternity ward where I had just lost my baby. I could see all the other pregnant women coming into the hospital to have their babies and this made me feel awful, as at that time, I was waiting for the post-mortem results on the death of my second baby. I felt so alone, and I felt that everything was on my shoulders. I was also in pain from the miscarriage, still grieving the loss of my baby, and my hormones were all over the place.

I saw all these other caring dads coming into the maternity wards in the morning to help their partners, and they brought in gifts, and extra clothes for them. I kept calling and calling my husband to try to talk to him, but he did not reply. I tried to be so resilient, but I was not coping. It was so hard as I was alone there. My daughter was crying, and she needed to be held down by me so that the doctors and nurses could take bloods and stuff, and do various tests on her. It was so emotionally and physically exhausting for me, and I was still bleeding heavily following the miscarriage.

Finally, I did get through to my husband and I said: *"Where are you? I need you."* and he just said: *"Oh, I forgot to set my alarm. I have only just woken up as I had a tiring night."* I was furious and so emotional. I remember going into the corridor crying, and I called my sister, as I did not know what else to do. I felt like I was just going to break in two. I was so overwhelmed, but I was still trying to put a brave face on everything (quiet pause). I could cry now just thinking back to the emotions that I was feeling at that time.

My husband then walks in the hospital, and he walks straight past me. He ignores me just like I did not exist. He didn't bring me any clothes or sanitary protection, no food, no money, or anything. In front of the nurses, he played with our daughter as if nothing had happened, but he was never there when he was really needed. After talking to my daughter, he just got up and deliberately walked straight past me saying that he had to go to town to sort out his mobile phone contract. I couldn't believe it. Sorting out his phone was obviously more important to him than being with me, and our daughter (pause). What a twerp! What a twerp! I felt so alone (heavy breathing).

When we came out of hospital, my friends offered to babysit my daughter so that my husband and I could go out together, but my husband did not want to go out, as he said that he was skint. My friends tried to persuade him to take me out for the evening. He liked Caribbean food and I had a free voucher for the restaurant, so I suggested to him that we could go there. My husband then said: *"You only want to go there because there is rum there."* He was trying to make out that I had a drinking problem.

I tried desperately to talk to him to get our relationship back on track, but when I tried to do this, he cruelly said: *"Every time you talk to me you just make my toes curl. I despise you. I hate your voice. I hate hearing you. I hate you ringing me. I cannot even look at you. You are disgusting! I don't love you anymore. I don't love you. We are just friends."* Hearing this, I realised that I did not love him anymore, and I said to him: *"Ok, let's break up then and let's do this amicably."*

Another friend of mine died soon after I lost the baby, and my daughter had just come out of hospital, and I was invited to a friend's party, which was a fundraising event for my friend who had died. My husband did not want me to go to the party and he just became so horrible. I told him that I wanted to go. He said that when I got back from the fundraising party we should break up. I decided to go to the party anyway, and I did get really drunk. I cheated on my husband with a man that I met there. I am not proud of it, but I can fully see now why it happened. I just really needed a cuddle. (Laughs).

When my husband found out that I had cheated on him, it was horrible. I did try to explain to him how I felt, but I could never get my husband to see this, as he was such a manipulator. We did split eventually, but just before this I found out that I was nine weeks pregnant, but I left him anyway, as I decided that I could not be with him anymore. I dreaded going home to him. I knew that I could not allow myself to be bashed about by him anymore. I used to cry when I got home from work.

We had an extremely messy break-up. We would argue a lot and he would go through my phone messages and accuse me of sleeping with different people and even one of his friends. He hacked into my social media account. I felt violated. During that time, we were still living together and he would go out on dates with other girls. Once I even lent him my car to take a girl out on a date (laughs). I just didn't care anymore as I had put everything into salvaging our relationship, and nothing had worked. He was trying to make me jealous, but it didn't work, as I had passed the point of caring anymore.

He finally met someone else, but she turned out to be not a very nice person. I had to get a Harassment Order against her in the end, as she was always messaging me and coming to my home and screaming outside. I don't know what he had told her. I then found out that she had had her own child removed from her care, and she had her driving licence taken away for drink driving, so I became very concerned for the safety of my children.

We ended up going to the court to sort out the care of the children. My ex accused me of stopping him from seeing his children. This was not true. I just needed some reassurance that his girlfriend was fit and able to look after my children properly. It turned out that she was given her own son back to care for, when he was 10 or 11 years old, so it must have meant that she was trying to make steps to get better. I think living with my ex helped her to get her son back as she now had a home to live in. Eventually, he split up with her too, when she was pregnant. It was like history repeating itself. Therefore, I had no sympathy for him when he came whining to me about his situation.

My daughter was 5 years old at the time and my ex would say things to her, and he would blame me for our marriage break up. He always made out that he was the victim, and he went round to all our friends looking for sympathy. He would message people and accuse me of being the one who broke up the family home. So, I was always walking on eggshells, even when he was not around. I just wanted him to move on.

Once he had moved out, he demanded that we had a DNA test done to prove that our child is his (laughs). My son is the image of his father though. There is no denying it, and I just laughed when he asked. I did let him come to the house to see the baby. He would stay overnight, and in the morning, he would come out of the room on his phone. He was always on dating apps, and that seemed to be his priority. That is when I realised that I did not want him being in my space at my home any longer. This is my safe haven now. He needed to grow up and begin to face his responsibilities of looking after the children.

When he started having the children to stay with him, he would bring my son back home with a dirty nappy, and tell me that he had not had time to change it! He told me that he could not have the children staying with him overnight anymore as he needed his sleep, and he had to get to work.

I really loved having my son on my own as a single mum. I loved it. It was the best. It was the most empowering experience, and I try to tell as many women as I can that they should not be frightened of being a single mum. It is fantastic. It is so much easier to manage the children on your own, without having a man to care for too. He was just like having another child to care for.

I realise now that it was the shame that silenced me and buried me. There seems to be a lot of shame around being a single mum, but this is wrong. These crazy 'societal norms' seem to govern us, but being a single mum is nothing to be ashamed of. It is something to be proud of. At least, you haven't got someone pulling you down every day, and criticising you all the time. I get very passionate about all of this. Women should congratulate each other, not compete with one another. Social media does not help. Everyone has struggles. It needs to be more real. I have a fierce inner strength now. My daughter is the same. She is a very fair empathetic child, but she will fight for what is right. I want to empower my children.

A friend of mine is going through a similar situation now with her partner, and the behaviour she is experiencing mirrors my own experience exactly. It's just crazy, but I find that now I can help her because I have been through similar experiences.

It has taken seven years of getting to the point now where my husband takes more care of the children and is sharing looking after them. It is now easier to manage who picks up the children. Oh, and my ex does not take part in pantomime performances anymore! (Laughs).

After my divorce, I met a boy at a festival. He was fun and into music and things. He had similar traits as my very first boyfriend. I tried hard to keep the relationship quite casual, but then he started 'love bombing' me. I made the same mistake again of being too open to him and confiding in him about my past. This was a big mistake. It was like handing him the ammunition to be able to use on me, to destroy me. Men like this are like predators – like Tyrannosaurus Rex waiting in the bushes to ambush you. They must loathe themselves so much to feel that they must treat us like that. I think he was one of the most dangerous men that I have ever met.

Initially, this man made me feel so special, so beautiful, so loved, and I felt that I was really wanted for the first time ever. I fell for him hook, line and sinker. I did have two little niggles in my mind about him though, and I should have listened to my instincts, but I didn't. At the time, I had a very distorted view of what 'real love' really was. He professed to me again and again, that he was such a good man, and that he would never do anything to hurt me. Now, I have learnt that you must be very wary of any man who says things like this to you. Ask yourself, why they would **need** to say this to you if they only have good intentions anyway.

These men are so nice to you in the beginning, but ultimately, I think they are trying to get information out of you. They are so shallow. They seem incapable of feeling anything. They must just copy the behaviours of others. They can break down in tears to get your attention, and you really believe that they are genuinely upset. They are very convincing and full of false promises, but underneath, they have no intentions of ever changing.

This boy (and I will call him a boy, not a man) I met was so dangerous, but he made me feel so good. He was so different to my husband. I felt loved and wanted, but I should have listened to my gut instinct.

Very soon in the relationship, he started to make negative comments on the clothes that I was wearing. His vicious comments were worse when he was drunk, but then he would blame the fact that he was drinking as the reason why he would say such things to me. He would suddenly wake up from sleeping and he would hit me. Then he would make an excuse that he had been dreaming. His behaviour got increasingly bad. I had two miscarriages with him. He got so nasty very quickly. His true colours came flying out. I wish I had ended it then.

People need to get educated on these behaviour traits and be able to look out for them so that they can recognise these traits as being a 'red flag' in the relationship. We need to develop good boundaries and have the confidence to report unacceptable behaviour.

This guy kept bringing up my past and taunting me about it. I found some Viagra in his bedside drawer and I asked him about it. He said that he used it because I had told him that I had been raped in the past. He said that knowing that I had been raped had put him off fancying me, and therefore, he needed to take the Viagra to sleep with me. This made me feel suicidal but having the children saved me.

I realised after this, that this guy was not right for me. I decided to check his phone, and I discovered messages on his phone that he had sent to other girls.

Once I was on the phone talking to my mother and he was listening in and he shouted out: *"Does your mum know that you were raped yet?"* This was so awkward for me as my mum heard what he had said, and she did not know anything about the rapes. He knew that she didn't know this too. It was so mentally cruel of him. My children were in bed at the time.

He was a rugby player, a hooker, and he pushed me into the kitchen and he pinned me down over the counter. His arm was across my throat and I scrabbled around with my hands to try to find something to hit him with. I found the knife block and he said: *"Do you think you are going to stab me?"* Then, he grabbed me by my hair, and he dragged me towards the tap, and he poured water in my mouth. He water boarded me. I couldn't breathe. I couldn't scream, or anything.

Then he pulled me down onto the kitchen floor, pinned me down and was strangling me, saying: *"You are just a piece of dirty Paki meat."* He said this because he knew that the people who raped me were Asian. I told him that he was no better than them, and he spat in my face. He said: *"I will show you,"* and he dragged me by my hair into the living room. I had carpet burns all down my legs. At that point, I thought he was going to rape me, and I was worried about my children upstairs. I passed out. When I woke up, I found my daughter standing over me saying: *"Mummy, Mummy! Mummy!"* He was there too, and he kept shouting at my daughter: *"She's lost her mind, she's lost her mind!"* I remember just seeing my daughter there, so I jumped up, grabbed her and I ran upstairs and I barricaded myself in her bedroom with my children. She was only seven years old at the time. I had no phone with me so I could not ring the police.

I got into her bed with her and I heard him pacing around outside the door and he kept repeating that he was going to put it on Facebook that I was a rape victim. I cowered down in silence. I felt such fear. I just stayed awake all night in the room with my children just listening to him going on and on. Then it went quiet, so he must have gone to sleep. Early in the morning, I took the children and I went to my sister's house.

I showed my sister the bruises on my body, and I explained to her what had happened. She did not know that I had been raped when I was younger either, so I had to tell her this to explain why he was attacking me. I told her that he was using information from my past as a tool to threaten me. I decided that I now needed to tell everyone what had happened to me just so he could not use this information to bully and threaten me anymore. I told my mum and my best friends about the rapes so that he could not have control over me anymore.

He then started ringing me, and he accused me of trying to stab him. I tried to get him to leave my house. I took my children out of the house to stay with friends of mine while he was there at my house collecting his belongings. As he was in the house gathering his stuff, he continued to threaten me. He pointed out the locks on the windows, and he told me that I should be careful as the locks were not safe and people could get in easily. He was just trying to make me feel fearful. He also said that he had copies of all the keys to my house. I made sure that I had taken all my important papers and passports, and then I left him there in the house to sort his stuff out.

When I went back later after he said he had left, I found all sorts of weird messages over the house. Things like old valentine cards that he had sent me in which he had written the word *'sorry.'* He even found an old diary of mine that I kept notes in while having therapy and he had written weird messages in there saying: *'now he has gone and he is so sorry, but you weren't listening to me.'* He began doing some very weird stalking behaviour, and he kept sending me threatening messages. He said that he needed to come back and collect more of his stuff from my house, so I offered to put it outside the house for him to collect, but he insisted on coming into my house, so I decided then to call the police. Once he found out that I was going to call the police, in a last effort to control me, he called my ex-husband and told him that I was on drugs and that I was not a good mother to his kids.

My ex-husband believed him. I approached my health visitor for help, and she understood the problem, and she was very supportive. Every day, I was on edge and I was always looking over my shoulder in fear, as he was constantly sending me threatening messages. My ex-husband kept communicating with him, which made it even more difficult for me, but my health visitor reassured me. She had lots of experience with these controlling and manipulative men, and she knew the sorts of things that they would attempt to do.

He used to try and contact me through other people, and he continued to try to control me. He would scare me, and he threatened to report me to Social Services to get my children taken away from me, but the health visitor stood by me. I felt so vulnerable, and I was on anti-depressants. His words really hurt. I remember that he used to tell me such awful things about his ex, saying that she was neurotic and crazy. I realise now that maybe these things he said about her were not true. He is the one who is crazy. I should have realised then what sort of person he was and how violent and volatile he was.

I did manage to get a Non-Molestation Order against him, but you need to report every little thing they do to achieve this. For example, he would damage my car, but it was hard to prove that it was him that did it. He was following me in my car all the time and stalking me, but again, it was hard to prove. The process was so time-consuming, but it did stop him for a while. Even when you do get a Non-Molestation Order, it does not always work. I had to get dash cams fitted in my car to try to get evidence of him following me. He would also get access into my 'YouTube' account, and he would post videos for me to see.

I suffered with PTSD after this. I blocked him on my phone and on social media, but he kept trying to contact me through other people and my friends. I was on a long waiting list for therapy. I eventually found a brilliant therapist who used EMDR on me which really helped.

After this, another male friend would write me long love letters and he once left a diamond ring on my doorstep in a deliberate attempt to get me to talk to him. He was waiting to get his feet under the table. He saw that I was vulnerable and he was yet another one who was trying to take advantage of me. He did take advantage of me when I was on sleeping tablets in the aftermath of my breakup with my previous partner.

There was a man who abused me when I was younger. We met on Facebook when I was 21. We had a brief relationship for around 6 months, but I thought that he was a weirdo and I had even blocked him on Facebook, but he got back in touch with me. He was more of a stalker. But I gave him a second chance. My girlfriend sort of enabled this relationship to develop as she told him: *"Louise is in a vulnerable place right now."* This just signalled to him that I was suitable prey.

I moved into his home, but by doing so, I lost everything. I lost my independence when I moved in with him. He would watch porn and stuff and there was one graphic video that he showed me from his phone. I was horrified when I saw it as it was so explicitly degrading of women. It was a video of a man sexually assaulting an unsuspecting young woman. He said that one of his employees had sent it to him on his phone. I could not believe that he could condone such a thing, and I told him so. He screamed at me when I challenged him. He would taunt me and he beat me up once. I reacted to him and I gave him a massive black eye and I left immediately. Because I hit him though, he got away with the abuse against me. My daughter witnessed most of this abuse, and therefore, she also had to have therapy.

My past does define me, and I did at one point think about killing myself, but it does not haunt me anymore. I have learnt so much and grown as a person. I am in a good relationship now, and I have been for a couple of years. It works well as we each have our own place and our own independent lives.

However, my doors are always locked now when I am in the house. I have dash cams in my car, in the front and the back just to detect if anyone is following me. My ex-partner knows the route that I drive to take the children to school and I still see him waiting to watch me, or he drives closely behind me. Everything goes through your mind at a hundred miles an hour about what might happen. I find myself driving different routes to avoid him, and I hide up different lanes to try to avoid him.

He broke his Non-Molestation Order. He got fitted with a tag for breaking his Non-Molestation Order, but in the day, he was free to go where he liked. He was always following me at the school pick-up time. I think he was trying to intimidate me and scare me. I have changed my phone number and my car to try to avoid him. Our daily family lives have become more restricted.

The hardest thing when reporting stuff like this to the police is gathering all the evidence. I did eventually do a video statement to the police about the rapes that had happened to me all those years ago, but as the perpetrator was living abroad by this time, he got away with this crime. If you decide to leave a man who abuses you, then you must make an exit plan. Don't tell them that you are leaving, as when they find out that you are leaving, then that is the most dangerous time of all.

(1) 'Gaslighting' is **a form of manipulation that often occurs in abusive relationships**. It is a covert type of emotional abuse where the bully or the abuser misleads the target by creating a false narrative and therefore makes them question their judgments and reality.

(2) The term **'flying monkeys'** is another way of saying **'abuse by proxy'** or having someone else do the bidding of in this case a narcissist.

(3) EMDR (Eye Movement Desensitisation and Reprocessing) is **a comprehensive psychotherapy that helps you process and recover from past experiences that are affecting your mental health and wellbeing**. It involves using side-to-side eye movements combined with talk therapy in a specific and structured format.

(4) 'Love bombing' is the practice of showing a person excessive affection and attention as a way of manipulating them in a relationship.

Life is a Pantomime

My life has been a pantomime,
With many ups and many downs.
I have learnt the pick-up lines,
And met these dangerous clowns.

They charmed me with their cheeky grins,
And I was really taken in.
They entertained me with their funny acts,
And love bombed me with glowing facts.

Control and power was their game.
To cause me hurt, and cause me pain.
The things they said were so untrue,
And they would beat me black and blue.

The emotional abuse tore me apart.
It broke my spirit and my heart.
Flying monkeys made it worse,
And looked upon me like a curse.

Now I lock my doors to keep them out
And if they come, then I will shout,
I do not need you in my life,
Go and find another wife!

No pantomimes are welcome here.
I want to make that very clear.
I've learnt my lesson that's for sure.
So don't come knocking at my door!

Melissa Stockdale
(2020)

2

AMANDA

'Living in Fear'

(Interviewed March 2022)

Amanda experienced domestic abuse for 14 years, from 1984 to 1998.

'I was always looking over my shoulder thinking
that something bad is going to happen.
I was still living in fear.'

I was just 20 years old, much too young, when I married John in July 1984. I knew him from school. I wasn't sure what I really wanted to do as a job, and I was a bit scared of the big wide world, so I stayed on at school and I did my A levels. I knew John from school days. He was a bit of a bad boy then. It might sound awful, but he was a bit thick as well (laughs). He wasn't really the type that I normally went for, but we began going out together. However, I was still unsure if he was really the right person for me. Even then, he was quite persuasive. I remember thinking then that he was not quite right for me, but he managed to smooth talk me around to not splitting up with him. He encouraged me to keep going out with him. We split up a few times, but he would always persuade me to go back to him.

John was in the army and based in Essex at the time. I was living in the Midlands. John said if we got married, we could then get our own army house together in Essex, rather than bothering to try to find a flat. Coming from a small town in the Midlands, the idea appealed to me, and I thought, ok I will go to see the big wide world. It was never a great love story between us. I just drifted into it you know. When I look back, I knew that my parents got married after knowing each other for only six weeks. They had a very loving relationship, and I had a great childhood, so I believed that it could also work for me, and I was looking for something like that.

I can remember the night before our wedding when John sent my friend up to ask if I was going to turn up to get married to him (laughs). Now I can see that this incident was a big red flag, but I did not notice it at the time.

We moved to Essex and it was more-or-less straight away that things started going wrong. I can't remember the first time that he ever hit me, but it was very early on and I remember running out of the flat and going to get on a bus to go home and he just came after me and grabbed me and said: *"You know that nobody will believe you,"* and he threatened me by saying that if I left, he would catch up with me and then it would be much worse. So, I went back to him, my poor, very naive 20-year-old self, (laughs, sighs), and that was it really.

I then got pregnant very early on in the marriage. I was working at the time. He obviously allowed me to go out to work. Then John told me that he would be going away to work in Cyprus for three months and he promised that he would be back home before the baby was born. Before he was due to leave, he said to me, *"Don't tell anybody at your work that I am going anywhere."* I replied, ok, even though I knew it was wrong to agree to this, but I just went along with it.

There was an older lady at work who was the same age as my mum and I confided in her that I was concerned that my husband was going away and that I would be alone, not really thinking that she would ever say anything. That day it was really tipping it down with rain, and John came to pick me up from work rather than me taking the two bus journeys that I normally had to take. He offered my friend a lift, and just as she got into his car, the first thing she said to John was: *"Oh, I hear that you are going to Cyprus."* My heart sank when she said this. When John heard her say this, I knew that it wouldn't be a good time for me. And sure enough, as soon as we got home, he became violent.

He would normally hit me across the back of the head, the tops of the arms or on the tops of the legs where it did not show or grabbed my hair. It was only when he lost control that I would get black eyes or stuff. Sometimes, if he did hit me in the face, he would break my glasses, and that was one of the worst things because I am so short-sighted. I remember feeling so annoyed and it really upset me. The number of times that I had to fix my glasses with superglue was unreal (laughs). I can laugh about it now, but at the time it was just horrendous. But I couldn't tell anybody. If I tried to go out to a phone box to phone my mum, he would always be there in the phone box with me. He didn't want us to have a phone at home, and this was in the time before we had mobile phones.

John was posted to Cyprus in May 1985. My 21st birthday was in June, and John suggested that I fly out to visit him at the Army base in Cyprus for six weeks or so. He promised me that he would be back home after three months. So, I flew over to Cyprus to see John. I had never flown before. It was a four-and-a-half-hour flight and it was in the days when smoking was allowed on airplanes. They had to change my flight to a daytime flight due to several hijackings that were happening around that time. When I arrived in Cyprus initially everything between us was ok, but after a week or so it began to get horrible again.

John had been given some leave, so he said that we should go somewhere. He wanted me to go on the back of a motorbike, which was reckless, bearing in mind that I must have been six months pregnant at the time. He said I could wear the crash helmet, but apart from this, he showed absolutely no care or concern for me at all.

I then went back to Essex at the end of July and John was supposed to be coming home to join me a couple of weeks later, but he called to say that the man who was going to cover for him for three months was not able to do so, and therefore he ended up staying in Cyprus for longer, until a couple of weeks before the baby was due. It was great for me as it was always better when John was not around. I question myself now, and I wonder why I did not leave him then and just go home to my mum, but for some reason, it never even entered my head to do that. It makes you realise how much these men get inside your head. My first daughter was born in October of that year and this is when things seemed to calm down a bit.

In 1987, John was posted to Germany. I was expecting my second child in June and we moved to Germany in the March. We drove from Zeebrugge all the way to West Germany. We slept in the car. I was pregnant and my daughter was only 17 months old, but John didn't even seem to care about this, or show any concern about me having to do all these things. I liked living in Germany, but the whole army living wasn't great as his postings were short. We lived in a flat most of the time. It wasn't a bad time though, as I had my daughter and my son, and I could speak a little German.

I fell pregnant again in 1988, but sadly I had a miscarriage in the September. It was horrendous. The medical staff at the Army base examined me and I was sent to hospital for a D&C. When I got sent back home from hospital after the operation, John was angry. The very first thing he said to me was: *"If you could have shown that you were more upset about your miscarriage, then the Army would have granted me more time off work to be at home to look after you."*

Yep, honest to God, that is what he said (laughs). Then he went straight back to work (quiet reflective pause).

My second daughter was born in July 1989. Shortly after this, John was posted to Ireland with the Army at one point, and I was allowed to have a phone then so that he could contact me. When he came back from Ireland, he was much worse, and he would complain to me that I did not send him enough letters to the army camp while he was away. He would make me feel guilty and bad by saying that the other men received lots of letters from their wives. He got very angry with me, and he didn't seem to understand that it was difficult for me with three small children to care for to be able to find extra time to send him more letters.

John was very self-centred and controlling. Day-to-day living was just awful. If the children woke up crying, he would always expect me to be the one to get up and look after them saying that he needed to get to work. He never once said sorry to me or felt any remorse for his actions. Even to this day, he has never said that he is sorry or admitted his abuse. I just wish he would admit it. I know John will never apologise to me. I don't need him to say 'sorry', I just want him to admit what he did.

I got called all sorts of names by John, and I thought at the time, I don't deserve this, but then I would doubt myself, and I would think, do I?

It is true what they say about emotional abuse being worse than physical abuse, as bruises heal quicker than a broken spirit. The cycle of abuse means that you do get to be able to anticipate when a physical attack is about to happen, but the day-to-day battering of your self-esteem is non- stop.

We moved a couple of times when we were in Germany. I would write to my parents and John always insisted on reading the letter before I sent it. At the time I did not think that this was unusual, but now I do. The idea of his controlling behaviour did not register with me then. If I telephoned my parents, he was always hovering behind me trying to listen in to what I was saying to them. He didn't really have a relationship with my parents. Whenever we went back to our hometown together, we always stayed at his mum's house, so we didn't see much of my mum and dad, which was wrong. It was so wrong (long pause).

I regret not letting my kids see my parents more, as my parents are both dead now. There are lots of things that I regret, but I can't do anything about it now. It was so hard (pause). If I had run off and left him early on in our relationship, I would not have had my children and I am thankful for them.

In 1993, we came back from Germany and we had to choose an Army base to live on for the last six months of his work. John refused to live in the area near my parents. He insisted on going back to Essex as he liked it there, but we were unable to get married quarters in that area, so we had to go to Suffolk. Which is where I live now and I do like it here. So that is a positive.

Things got much worse when John left the Army. He took a lump sum, and redundancy after his time in Iraq and he wanted to buy a new Mazda estate car. He wanted me to drive his Ford Sierra car back from Germany, but I had not got a driving licence, so I had to take lots of driving lessons. When I failed my driving test, strangely John did not seem to get annoyed about it. This was the one time I really expected him to get annoyed, but he didn't. This is surprising now, thinking about it. But I think he didn't want me to have my own car anyway as having a car would then enable me to have some freedom.

We bought a house in Suffolk after six months in married quarters, and I got a job at a supermarket. John had done his six months rehabilitation and he got a job as a lorry driver, and then a job in a warehouse.

John made all the decisions and he used to go out whenever he wanted. He could make friends easily and he was always going out for a drink. It was the army mentality and something that he had been encouraged to do as a soldier in the form of 'sports afternoons' every Friday. He tried to transfer this habit over to his civilian work and he would go out drinking with the boys on a Friday night, in the hope that doing this on a regular basis would help him to get promoted at work. Things carried on as 'normal' with him accusing me of having affairs at work, waiting outside to pick me up from my place of work, then attacking me when we got back home at home, particularly if I was late coming out of work. John would shout at me accusingly by saying: *"Who have you been talking to? What is his name?"* There were also times when John would send the children up to their rooms and then he would close the sitting room curtains. This was a signal to me, which meant that I had said the wrong thing, and therefore I would be getting a beating for it. He would get annoyed at the slightest thing.

His mum moved down to where we lived, and she got herself a little house nearby. She would look after the kids, which was very helpful as we both worked odd hours. John always expected his mum to do this, and he didn't bat an eyelid about how she seemed to only be doing this to please him. He was very disrespectful to her, and he would call her names. I have even seen John kick his own mum before.

:d away last year. John's father died from a massive
.ck when John was just a teenager and John and his
ᴠ……ᴇ· always blamed their mum for not giving their father
CPR to try to save him when he had this heart attack. They
accused their mum by saying: *"You let our dad die."* They
never let their mum find a boyfriend after that, so she was
always on her own. I felt a little bit sorry for her, but she did
kind of let her own children walk all over her.

John did not behave any differently towards me, even
when his mum was around. The day we finally split up and
I kicked him out of the house, his mum was staying with us
and babysitting the children. She saw what was happening,
and she just said to me, *"What have you done to John now?"*

When I was working at the supermarket, I had made
quite a few friends at work, but I would never introduce
them to John. I had a few male friends at work, but I prayed
that John would not come into the shop and catch one of
these men talking to me. It just wasn't worth it, as I knew
when I got home, he would be angry and he would ask lots
of questions about how long I had known them, ask me
why they were talking to me, and ask if I was sleeping with
any of them. He was constantly accusing me of having
affairs. I am not sure where he thought I would find the
time or the energy to do this.

We would have arguments where he would demand sex,
but I was often too tired and I just wanted to go to sleep,
but then we would have a big argument and he would twist
the words around that I was saying, and I realised that it
would be easier to just give in and have sex with him. After,
having sex he would then accuse me of the time that had
been wasted on arguing.

There were many times that he would make me sleep on the floor if I refused to have sex. I remember one time that I was laying there on the floor thinking and promising to myself that I will not be doing this when I am forty years old. I kept saying to myself that I would leave him when I reached forty, as my youngest would be 15 years old by then. So, I had it all planned in my head about what I was going to do, and I knew that it was not going to be like this forever.

Once, I did kick him out of the house before I was forty years old, but it was a very hard thing to do, as he would threaten to do things to me if we ever split up. For example, he once said: *"If you try to leave me, I will throw you off the Orwell Bridge and I will tell people that you had killed yourself."* I was really scared because I believed everything that he said. I stayed with him, as I feared what he would do to me, and he was a big bloke.

There was one incident that polarised everything. My son had started at his secondary school, and he couldn't tie his tie properly and John began yelling at him. He was always yelling at the kids. John was trying to get my son to do his tie up, but then he suddenly slapped my son hard around the head and my son fell over on the floor. Seeing this, I decided that this was the final straw. I did not do anything about this at the time, but I did begin to wonder and worry what John might be doing to the kids when I was not around.

My youngest did tell me that John forced them to eat mashed potato once when I wasn't there, and he was shoving it in their faces. The children still see their father now even though they are all adults. I am not sure how I feel about this some days, as I think that John does not deserve them, but he is their father after all.

On the night that everything came to a head, I wonder if subconsciously I had already decided that this would be it. There would be no going back because I really thought that he would kill me. John and I went out together somewhere. I was drinking, and I had got a little bit tipsy. When we got back home, we started arguing and he pushed me, so this time I retaliated and I kicked him in his groin. This is the only time that I have ever fought back, but this only made matters worse. John went for my face and he really started hitting me hard. His mum, who was babysitting at the time, must have heard the noise and she came downstairs and she sent John up to bed, which he did after throwing all my clothes down the stairs. I was lying on the sofa and I fell asleep there, but I woke up suddenly to find his hands around my neck. This was the first time he had ever done that. He then went upstairs again.

I woke up early the next day, which was a Sunday morning and I was supposed to be at work, so I quickly got dressed and I went to work. John must have heard me leave the house because he followed me in his car. I saw him following me, so I ran all around the houses through the estate to arrive at work. Then I saw him driving in the car park. He shouted out of his car window saying: *"Sorry, it won't happen again."* I banged on the staff entrance door at work and thankfully my friend at work let me in. She could see all my bruises, and I told her to call the police, which she did.

My friend went with me to the police station and they took loads of pictures of my face and everything. While we were there, we heard John being brought into the station by the police, as they had arrested him. He started crying, and he was saying: *"Why is this happening to me?"* That was it for me. I never let him back in the house again. He obviously saw the kids though.

After I had written my statement and given it to the police, John phoned me up and he threatened me again, saying: *"You do know that if you give in that statement, this case will go to court and it will be in the papers, and the kids will get bullied at school."* This made me worry about my children, and I knew that I had to think twice because of the effect it would have on the kids.

Stupidly, I withdrew my statement to the police and I wonder now why I did this, but John still went to court anyway, and he was charged with ABH (Actual Bodily Harm). He got a suspended sentence and he got let off. I went back to work after that and my friend at work came to me and said: *"You will never guess who is outside laughing and joking?"* It was John. I realised then that reporting him had not made the slightest bit of difference.

I now had the problem of caring for the kids and selling the house. John was unable to keep paying the mortgage, so effectively I was homeless. I was put in a halfway house until the authorities could find me a place to live, which is where I am now. I ended up with hardly anything.

I still wanted the kids to have a relationship with their dad if they wanted to. I knew that it was important for them to do this, as I always had a very good relationship with my dad. My children were 10, 12 and 14 years old at the time, and they would all go off to see him. When they returned, they told me that their dad had got a new girlfriend, but that they had been told by him not to tell me. Apparently, he had been seeing her for months before we had split up. I felt disgusted and cheated, particularly as John had treated me so badly, and he had constantly accused me of being the one who was cheating, but still, he did not have the decency to tell me that there was someone else in his life.

John and his new girlfriend then moved away out of the area, and the kids used to go and stay with them. John told me soon after this, that he thought that he should have full custody of the children as he could provide for them better than I could. I told John that he could take me to court. He did then take me to court where I felt that I was failed by the system.

A court warden had meetings with me and visited me at my home with my kids, and they also visited John with the kids, I told them that John would lie and try to bribe them, and he would also bully the kids into staying with him. I asked the court warden to make sure that what I was saying to them was recorded. However, my words were not recorded or even considered by them, and therefore this was not brought up at all in the court proceedings.

I realise now that if someone can talk the tale, they can manipulate the court system and get away with it. John made out he was a decent man, and he used the fact that he had been in the army to present himself to the court as a 'good' man and therefore he managed to persuade them to believe him.

As John was the one who brought the court action against me, it also meant that I had to make long journeys and travel a distance to where he lived, to attend all the court cases. When I wrote my statement, I put in all about the domestic abuse that I had endured. My statement was read out in the court proceedings in front of his new girlfriend, and I could see on her face that she had no idea about the abuse. I am sure John told her that I was lying as she is still living with him now.

My two youngest children went to stay with him, which broke my heart, but I still saw them on a regular basis. I never got over the feeling though that I had let them down. I've always had a good relationship with my children. In conversation once with my son, he once said to me: *"You do know that we never blamed you."* I should hope not, I thought, but anyway, it was nice to hear them say this, as I am sure they were told some right tales about me from their dad.

The children still have a relationship with their dad and they seem to just accept the situation. They often say to me: *"You know what he is like mum."* I hate it when they say that to me. It infuriates me.

I don't see John unless it is an event that the kids have organised. I can be civil to John, but I usually avoid him. I cannot forgive and forget what happened, so I do not engage in conversation with him.

Now that I am working to help others suffering domestic abuse, I feel like I really own my past lived experience. It might sound petty, but I want my ex-husband to know that I am doing this job. Going through my own experience has now got me into doing a purposeful and rewarding job that I love, and I want him to know this. I have no idea what John is doing now.

When I look back, I think it was the threatening behaviour that made life so difficult for me. After we split up, my friends invited me to go out and socialise with them, but I was not relaxed when I was out. I was always looking over my shoulder thinking that something bad is going to happen. I was still living in fear.

I think the worst thing of all was telling my mum and dad what had happened. That was horrible. Shortly before we split up, my mum was around 70 then I think, and she was about to have her gall bladder removed, so I arranged to go and see her. John told me I had to take one of the kids with me, as he didn't want me to go out anywhere on my own. He always thought that I would be meeting up with other blokes on the train or something. So, I took my daughter.

My dad met me off the train and that is when I eventually admitted to him about what had happened between John and me. My dad was devastated, and he wondered why I had not told him before. He said that if I had, then he could have helped me. My dad said that he would have broken John's legs if he had known what he had done to me. I asked my dad, as a favour, if he could please tell my mum. So, he did. My mum was shocked and crying when she found out, as she believed that everything was fine.

Although, I found it difficult to tell my parents, my friends at work who helped me obviously knew something was wrong, and I am sure that those who did not know at work had already guessed. The neighbours must have known. I am sure they must have known, but people just don't want to get involved. I also recognised that involving others can sometimes make it worse, particularly if you are not ready to leave.

When I eventually kicked John out, I did get a call from Victim Support, but that was the only support that I ever got. There was nothing there to support me (pause). Maybe there was (pause), but no one ever told me. In the late 1990's there was no way to find help. I often wonder if things would have been different if I had the right help and support available at that time. If I had been able to engage with somebody to help me then, I would have got out of the situation much quicker.

When I look back, I just remember myself lying on that bedroom floor desperate to find a way out. I remember how worthless I felt then (pause). I now find that I have great empathy with others who suffer similar things. It was a female officer at the local police who really helped me.

The abuse that I endured happened over a very long period until I divorced in 1998, and this has affected me for a large part of my life. I sometimes wonder what it would have been like if it hadn't happened, but then I would not be doing the job I do now, which I love. After my own experiences, I am now able to truly help others who have also been victims of domestic abuse.

Red Flags

You make excuses for his behaviour
You defend him to your friends
You feel uneasy but you do it
You always try to make amends.

You feel that you might lose him
So you forgive him for his lies
He blames you for his problems
And you accept his faults and try.

You let him insult you often
About your looks and things you've said
He uses sex to control you
He becomes demanding in the bed.

You allow him to compare you
To other people in his life
You tolerate his behaviour
Because now you are **his** wife.

He thinks that he now owns you
To do whatever he desires
You do your best to comfort him
And put out angry fires.

You change your own expectations
And ignore his violent rage
You think if you dismiss his anger
He will calm down and turn the page.

You apologise and placate him
As you fear what he might do
This will not solve the problem
As his aim is to destroy you.

The red flags are there for a reason
Take heed and listen hard
Seek help and a safe haven
Watch out! Be on your guard.

Melissa Stockdale
(2020)

3

NIKI
Part One: 'The Truth Will Out'

(Interviewed June 2022)

*'One day, I thought that the only way of
getting help or making it stop
would be to end my own life.'*

I endured a two-year terror of stalking and I had prepared
myself for the trial of a **4A Stalking Offence: 'Stalking
involving fear of violence or serious alarm or distress'
(1)** in the hope that finally the torture would end, and I
would be free. Instead, the trial was vacated. I took photos
of myself on this day, before and after the trial and they
visibly show the dramatic effect that this news had on me.

After a court hearing in February 2022, the perpetrator
manipulated evidence and submitted a psychologist report
stating that he was 'unfit to plea' and therefore needed an
intermediary. He did this in a deliberate attempt to claim
that he was unfit to stand trial. However, the Judge
overruled and the trial date was set for June 2022.

The court allowed me to attend this court hearing, via a
video link from my home following how the proceedings
affected my mental health before. A criminal court
Independent Domestic Violence Advisor was due to come
to my home to support me through the trial, as I now have
a stammer caused by the trauma and the stress. I thought at
last that the waiting would be over, but then I was notified
at the last minute that the trial would again be delayed for
another three months.

Many people fear that being a stalking victim makes you
weak, and some people are too embarrassed to say that it
happened to them. Please never be. My advice would be:
*"Remember, that you are the most beautiful, resilient, intelligent
individual ever, and it can happen to anyone at all, no one is
immune, but on this occasion, it just happened to be you."*

You see, over the last two years, the postcode lottery saw a system fail me, and not just me, but also my family. The police kept saying to me that there was nothing more they could do. The children's services classified it as 'civil', but the sheer terror and fear that I now live in is something that I would never wish upon anyone else.

I moved. I had no choice because there was no help and support out there. Stalkers are amazing at manipulating things, and cleverer than people can ever imagine. They can make you think that you are over-reacting. They make you feel guilt that they may kill themselves and that it will be your fault if they did. Stalkers find ways to get to you physically and psychologically. When they can't get you, they then go after your friends, and your family, so that you become isolated. This is when you begin to isolate yourself. To protect yourself, you don't go out. You shut yourself off from the outside world just to protect others, as you soon realise that anyone who has helped you has now unfortunately become a target.

One day, I thought that the only way of getting help or making it stop would be to end my own life. The services were not helping to make the stalking stop, and I thought that if I died, then there would be a case review, and all the failings and lack of support from the services would be uncovered and then maybe lessons would be learnt. I believed that this might prevent the same happening to anyone else. Also, my friends and family would then be safe, and finally, my children would get some support.

Eventually, from the prolonged psychological trauma, I have become not only a silenced victim; but I was silenced even more when I developed a **psychogenic stammer (2)** (Yes it really exists). That's when I thought he had won.

When I received the official diagnosis of a 'psychogenic stammer' which had derived from the prolonged trauma sustained from my stalking, I was asked the question: *"What do you think was the breaking point for why it happened?"* I gave a very clear answer: *"I fully believe that the breaking point for me was between February 2020 and February 2021. Had the children's services not classified my case as 'civil' and the police had not said to me that 'he was on the tenancy and had a legal right to be at the house."* These events prolonged and significantly intensified my trauma.

I honestly think if I'd have been given the right support at the right time, and I had not been left to fend for myself for a whole year, then this may not have happened. Proper support would have eased my mind and would have helped to relieve some of the strain that I was going through, but now it's too late. I've been told that my stammer is not curable, and it can go for days, weeks, months or years. There is nothing I can do about this life-changing consequence, which I believe is entirely due to a lack of relevant services being available, and the proper support provision being in place for victims of this type of offence.

The day when the terror should have finally ceased would have been my first day of freedom, but it was not to be, and I just wanted to give up. I was so very tired of fighting the same old battles day in and day out. I did not give up though because I realised that if I did give up being a living stalking victim, I would not be able to speak out and show the world the real impact of what stalking can really do to people, and explain how little help there is currently out there to help people like me. Some victims, like the young beautiful Gracie Spinks who was murdered by her stalker, did not get the choice of giving up; so, I realised that if I gave up, I would feel like I am letting her down and other people like her, who never got the choice of whether to keep going or to give up.

'Gracie's Law' and the charity **'Stalking Victims Support UK'** are so important. There is a real lack of service provision for victims of stalking and this needs to change. That is why I support these organisations. This support could potentially save lives. I cannot reverse my new speech impediment, which I now must accept and live with, but what I can do, is speak out on behalf of others to show where support is needed. So please if anybody is looking at fundraising, or people want to make a difference, the charity is much needed, and a good place to start.

I met my husband in a pub in early 2008 via some friends. I was pregnant with my second child at the time. He played 'World of Warcraft' with my friends online and they had arranged to meet up with them. I eventually lost connection with these friends, as my partner deliberately turned me against them. He told me that my friends thought that I was a *'cocky, arrogant cunt'* and that they didn't like me, so we stopped seeing them.

Initially, the relationship with my partner was great. I would come home from work and the ironing would be done, but he refused to find any employment. He kept telling me that his dad had said that he didn't have to work. He was concerned about getting fleeced by the CSA (Child Support Agency) to pay maintenance for his son if he worked. He described to me how his ex-partner, the mother of his son was a bit 'psychotic'. He told me that she denied him having any contact with their child, so he did not see why he needed to pay for him.

Eventually, he did find a job as a salesman in a store, which he seemed to enjoy. However, within five months of us being together, rows started to happen and the 'honeymoon' period seemed to be over. He threatened to leave me. I was very upset and I remember that he rang his place of work and he told them that he would not be going to work that day as I had gone into premature labour. This was untrue. My daughter was born two months later.

A week after the birth of my daughter, we moved into my father's pub and we lived rent-free in the flat above. My mum employed my partner as the pub manager, but rather than working or dealing with the beer deliveries, he would instead, spend his time playing 'World of Warcraft'. He expected me to manage running the pub even though I was still on maternity leave and looking after a new baby.

I was absolutely shattered and emotionally worn down. My mother became increasingly worried about me, and she was upset when she witnessed how he treated me. She mentioned to him that he should begin to pull his weight a bit more and support me. This resulted in him falling out with my mother. He then gave me an ultimatum, saying that either I move back with him to his father's house, or our relationship would be over.

I felt emotionally torn and extremely guilty, as my mum had only been trying to do us a favour. I was worried about the conflict between us, and I felt that it was my fault. I left the next day with my partner, and then I lost contact with my mother for a while. He forbade me from talking to my mother, as he did not like her. If my parents did visit us, he would ignore them. He would continue to play games on his computer or shout at me, and the children in front of my parents. This hatred towards them continued throughout our relationship. He was so toxic towards my parents that they eventually stopped coming round to see us.

We lived with his father for a while whilst looking for a home of our own. His ex-partner, who was the mother of one of his sons, had also recently given birth to a baby and she lived close by. He told me that she was struggling to cope as the baby was keeping her awake all night, so he would go to visit her often and assist with his son's morning school run, leaving me to cope alone.

He worked out the finances, and he calculated all the money that I was earning. He pointed out that he wouldn't need to get a job, as then he would have to pay the CSA for his other son. He said that if he had to do that, then he would basically not have any wages left so it was pointless for him to be working.

In February 2009, a new iPhone came out and he gave me another ultimatum; either I buy him the new iPhone, or I leave. He knew at this point that I had nowhere to go, because my mother and I were no longer on speaking terms due to us letting her down regarding the pub, and I had my two children to think about and care for.

Reluctantly, I gave up and I bought him the iPhone despite only receiving statutory maternity pay, very little child benefit, and tax credits. His brother, who overheard his threat about the phone, thought it was a big joke. He called him 'Andy Pandy iPhone'.

I paid for our two phone bills. We had two contracts, one in my name and one in his. Each year, a new iPhone was released and he would always have to have the latest model. He would upgrade the contracts whether it was his or mine. He would then take the new phone, and I would get the old 'hand me down' phone from him. It was not worth arguing with him, or saying 'no' to him, as I knew there would be recriminations.

My partner's father acted as a guarantor, and he lent us a bond so that we were able to get our own house. I handed in my resignation, and I found a higher-paid job. While I was working, my partner continued to play 'World of Warcraft' all through the night, and then he would sleep all day. He would help his ex-partner by doing the morning school runs for their son, but I was expected to organise my children and drop them off at nursery as well as working full time. I discovered later, that he was inviting his ex around to our house, and running errands for her, while I was working and funding everything. In the meantime, he was not working, nor looking after the children.

I struggled to work out how I could juggle everything, and this is when depression set in. I felt so low and tired. My partner's temper had manifested itself, and he would continually shout and belittle me. He would demand that I make him food, like cheese on toast, whenever he needed it. His son, (who often stayed with us weekends) would start to imitate his father's behaviour, and then do the same. It became intolerable. There were times when I had cooked him food, and he would spit it out on the plate in front of me, and in front of the children, saying that it was *"disgusting"* or not cooked to his liking.

We moved in with two of our friends and we lived with them for a while until September 2009 when we moved into our own home. My partner became self-employed, but I ended up being the one to run the business, making calls, and going to meetings, while he just did some basic computer work. He continued to play computer games all night, and then he would sleep in the day. I became depressed again, and my GP referred me to a counsellor.

My partner insisted that I stop speaking to our friends who had helped us move house. He told me that he was concerned that they were trying to match me up with her brother, who was newly single. It was much easier for me to agree not to speak to them again, rather than be verbally reprimanded by him.

In December 2009, my husband told me that to *'save our relationship'* he was going to live at his dad's house during the week and he would only be home with me and the children at weekends. Throughout this time, I was still trying to run his business, which was difficult, as he would only allow me to contact him at certain periods of the day. He was out socialising with his friends while he was staying at his dad's house. When I could not get hold of him, he would tell me that he had accidentally fallen asleep at a friend's house, or say his phone battery was dying.

To continue running his business, I had to pay for the children to attend nursery. He had taken the car with him, so I also had to pay to transport them there. I missed attending my counselling sessions, as it was hard to get to the centre without a car. I also gave my husband money for travelling to and from his dad's house each week.

It seemed very odd when he asked me to pay for his accommodation, particularly when he was with his dad, so I checked his Facebook messages, and this is when I found out that he was seeing another girl who he had known from school days. He told her that I was a *'psychopath'* and that I was his *'ex'*. When I confronted him, he moved out, and he went back to his dad's house, but three days later he rang me. He was crying, and saying sorry, so I took him back. I don't think he ever spoke to the girl again.

The following year, I became pregnant with his baby and we moved to a new home. Our son was born later in 2010 and we moved to yet another property later that year, then we had another son together in 2012. After this, I started a new job as a medical secretary and we had two more children who were born in 2014 and 2016. In 2017, I went back to college to study. In 2018, my husband's son from his previous relationship came to live with us, and I began training to become a midwife.

During our whole relationship, he constantly called me names and he belittled me until by self-esteem dropped to rock bottom. He was always weight-obsessed and this behaviour rubbed off on me. I began to think that I also weighed too much. He was rarely employed, and the pressure was always on me to pay for things we needed. I also had to pay off his debts when he borrowed money from friends. I did this to avoid conflict and arguments.

He would always make me feel guilty for going out with friends. The guilt that I was made to feel often resulted in me making excuses to refuse invitations from friends or find reasons to explain why I could not go. He closely monitored and controlled how long I was away from the house. I remember once, that I was in my car on the phone, crying to my friend, following a time when he had physically assaulted me in front of the children. After the call, I nipped into a local shop that was around the corner from our house. I was only gone from the house for half an hour, but when I returned home, he accused me of being out much longer, and of speaking to men on my phone.

Once in 2018, I attended a friend's hen party. He continuously sent texts to me throughout the evening. I consumed far too much alcohol that night and I felt sick when I came home. I curled up on the bathroom floor. He came into the bathroom and took pictures of me in jest. He accused me of being unfaithful to him and he said that on the CCTV I was not wearing my leggings when I got home, so obviously I had *'fucked someone'* whilst I was out. I had in fact come home in my leggings and I was still wearing them.

The amount of grief that I suffered for going out with friends meant that it really was not worth going out with them again. When I was out alone, I would be constantly messaged by him and told off if I turned the **'Life360'** off on my phone.

He would often accuse me of being unfaithful. If I spoke to any men or had any male friends, he would say that I had *'fucked'* some of the people that I was talking to. One friendship where I was accused of being unfaithful, was with a gay male friend who worked in the same department as me. We used to smoke together outside during our lunch break. I tried to explain this to my partner, but he pointed out to me that it doesn't have to be a loving relationship to be *'cheating'*, and cheating can come in the form of giving someone else your time, or by sending messages. I stopped messaging and hanging around with my friend at work due to the amount of grief I got from my partner for speaking to him.

My partner also became angry and accused me of *'fucking'* some people who I chatted to on a Facebook group. They were members of the Army Cadet Force that I belonged to 20 years ago. We were only sharing old photos and arranging a reunion online. This is an example of what would happen if I spoke to any men, or had any male friends.

My husband was very much into **BDSM (3)**, and sexually I found myself in a vicious cycle. At first, it was low-level, and it included getting dressed into various outfits and using the occasional sex toy, but it became increasingly worse than that. He would like to video everything, and

because I did not always want to do something, it ʼ
often hurt. It became a cycle of him saying that he w......eu
it, me saying no, then us having a domestic argument until
I finally said yes. Then he would want to use x, y, and z, and
I would say no, so he would belittle me, and call me boring
until I said yes. I remember once that I was crying during
sex, so he stopped and then told me off for crying. He
would expect sex every two days, and if I didn't comply,
then I was accused of avoiding him.

Eventually, I started trying to work more night shifts to
avoid the night times with him because I simply did not
want to have sex every day. He would expect me to walk
around the house with no knickers on under my skirt, or
ask me to go out in public to parties with him with love eggs
inserted in my vagina. If I refused, he would become
verbally abusive towards me. He threatened to join **'Tinder'**
to find sex elsewhere if I did not comply. If I had a work
shift, he would quickly take me into the bathroom for his
own satisfying five minutes, and I would oblige even if it
hurt me, just so that I didn't have to listen to the verbal
aggression or be told again by him that I was boring.

Anyone who has ever spoken out or tried to defend me
has also come under his firing line. He tried to have my dad
arrested for theft of some items from my garage that either
never existed, or that he had already in his possession. He
also made false allegations against my mother at her place
of work, for which she was investigated and cleared, but
obviously, this investigation took several months and it was
very distressing for everyone.

He was very paranoid in general. He installed multiple
pieces of CCTV and surveillance equipment around the
house to spy on me. During the day he would log into the
CCTV to check up on me. He would use excuses like he

was checking to see if the gardener had cut the lawn, but after we broke up a friend of mine admitted that she was with him a few times when he when he was checking up on me via his phone. She witnessed him doing these checks, and he would also tell her what he was doing. She thought that this was very odd behaviour, but she did not want to say anything to me at the time, as she did not wish to cause any problems in the relationship between us or be responsible for the breakdown of our relationship.

I split up with my husband in February 2020 and between that time and June 2020, he continuously stalked me to the point where there is now a trial for **'4A Stalking'** **(2)** He would contact me on every platform, 50-100 messages a day. When I blocked him on one device, he'd then find the next: text messages, **'Whatsapp'**, **'Facebook'**, **'Snap chat'**, email; and do you know you can even text an email address on **'iMessage'**?

He would dial into the **'Ring Doorbell'** and the **'Alexa'**, to listen to what was going on in the house where I lived, and if I mentioned to a friend that I was going to the shop to buy something, then he would turn up with the item that I wanted to buy within half an hour.

He moved onto the next street to mine, and he would come round 2-3 times a day uninvited to just 'drop in' he said. The police said that they could not stop him doing this as his name was on the property tenancy agreement, so he had a legal right to be there.

He started sending me unwanted gifts, designer bags, flowers, get-together anniversary presents, even though we were not together. He threatened to commit suicide, and he sent me pictures of himself crying.

My friend and I created a 'goof' **'Tinder'** account and it only took him four hours after we had made it, for him to find it. This just shows how obsessive and persistent he is.

He would use the kids as tools against me. When I tried to move house, he applied through the family court for prohibitive steps to stop me moving. There was no escape.

When he had a stroke, he told everyone in the village that I was the cause of it.

He referred to me on social media, but his actions did not breach the non-molestation order that was in place, as it said *"mother of my children"* and he did not use my actual name.

At one point he played our wedding song repeatedly on the **'Alexa'** in the house, and when I kept stopping it, it would then start again. He had a 'take away' delivered to my house, saying that he had *'forgotten that he had moved.'*

He imitated a doctor, and he wrote to my place of work, and my university telling them that I needed to be removed from practice immediately for breaking the current 'lockdown rules', and he gave out my best friends' names and addresses within this email.

When I got a 'Non-Molestation Order' against him, he went mad at the hearing, and he then applied to a higher court to have it discharged. He convinced the police that he wasn't mobile, and because of this, he managed to have his bail conditions dropped. This enabled him to pass through my street again, prior to the non-molestation order being granted.

He would indirectly refer to me across social media, so I was identifiable by reference but not by my name. This was not considered as a breach of the order. One example was that one of my kids bumped his head at school, but his social media post implied that I had done it. Consequently, I received grief from the public.

One day, I noticed that my **'Facebook'** messages had been read, and it turns out that he had been logged into my social media account on his **'iPad'** and **'Safari'** for years. He would track me using the **'Apple ID'** so I had to lock him out of it by getting a friend to set a secret password and remove his devices. Another day he came round and I had changed the pin number on my phone, but he was desperate to get hold of it. It turns out that you can change your pin, but if the **'Face ID'** is still active, it will override that, and he had set my phone up so that his face could unlock it too.

He used to dial into the router in my house to see what devices were attached to it, to see if I was alone. He would also call the older kids on **'Skype'** to ask them to open the house, and let him in.

I purchased a new **'Ring Doorbell'** and he asked me if it was for him. He then showed me why it wouldn't work. He said: *"watch this"* then he proceeded to walk from the end of the drive towards the doorbell, and he put his hand over the camera and explained to me that it only records the first 30 seconds after motion is detected, unless the doorbell button is pressed.

He had CCTV cameras erected all around the top of my house and my dad kept pointing them away, so he then threatened to have my dad charged with criminal damage for touching his stuff. As my husband was listed on the tenancy, the police said that there was nothing that they could do, as the cameras were legally partially owned by him even though he had a tenancy registered elsewhere. As a single claimant on 'Universal Credit', I only got half the payment for the rent help that I was entitled to, as it was a joint tenancy.

He tried to have me charged for stalking him, by saying that I was driving past his house, but I was at work. Fortunately, I had multiple witnesses and concrete proof that I was at work during this time of the Covid pandemic.

He would use his friends and family to contact me and give me grief. He had access to all the parental controls on kids' 'Nintendo' switches, and their phones, and he blocked them all so that I would then have to contact him for the passcodes. He kept begging me to go to his house with the kids for dinner. Also, when he came to the house to collect the kids, he kept trying to hug me, and stuff.

He sent me naked pictures of himself including genitalia, saying that he needed to lose weight. He also put a naked photo of me on his phone. He has an **'iPhone'** and he would say to me that he couldn't stop himself from unlocking his phone, as where he had to swipe the screen up, it happened to be right on my vagina. He put naked pictures of me on the display screen of his own **'Amazon Echo'** at his house, and then he sent me a picture of it. He would get his penis out and waggle it. One day when he came to get the kids, I went to put their stuff in his car boot just to get out of his way, but then he came up behind me, and he bent over me so that his penis rubbed against me.

I've ended up eventually moving, but now he is manipulating the family court reports to imply that I'm incapable of parenting.

The impact this had had on me, from experiencing his stalking, the abuse, and trying to achieve justice is suicide attempt, self-harming, agoraphobia, complex PTSD, depression and extreme anxiety. This has also resulted in an eating disorder and a psychogenic stammer. I have never had a speech problem before. It is so bad that they had to rule out that it was a stroke. I've ended up on a 'Blue Badge' and I cannot even go out to the shops alone now.

People often ask me, *"Why did you stay with him if he was abusive?"* I wish they could understand that leaving an abusive partner puts the victim into an even more dangerous situation. This process poses the highest risk to the victim. There is a very useful film clip and TED talk that has been suggested by Women's Aid that clearly explains why women stay in abusive situations.

This is available to watch at: www.womensaid.org.uk

(1) 4A Stalking Offence:
https://www.legislation.gov.uk/ukpga/1997/40/section

Information on levels of stalking:
https://www.gov.uk/government/publications/a-change-to-the-protection-from-harassment-act-1997-introduction-of-two-new-specific-of

(2) A psychogenic stammer is often caused by fear, mistrust and betrayal and the persistence of intrusive and distressing recollections. This is a specific form of PTSD. The stammer persists as a form of protection against experiencing the fear again, and it is triggered by specific stimuli in the person's surroundings that are related to the original event. Openly sharing a narrative of the fearful event can help overcome the stammer.

(3) BDSM is a variety of erotic practices or roleplaying involving Bondage, Discipline, Dominance and Submission, Sadomasochism and other related interpersonal dynamics.

For anyone suffering from sexual assault, information and support can be found at any Sexual Assault Referral Centre (SARC)
https://www.nhs.uk/service-search/other-services/Rape-and-sexual-assault-referral-centres/LocationSearch/364

NIKI

Part Two: 'Fighting for Justice'

(Interviewed for the second time November 2022)

Niki is still living in fear for her life, as her stalker remains at large. She is currently working closely with the police trying to secure an **SPO - Stalking Protection Order (1).** SPOs were established in early 2020, after the brutal murder of Alice Ruggles who was killed by her stalker in 2016. Following her death, Alice's parents set up a charity to increase public awareness about the risks of stalking, and they also initiated a campaign in the UK to introduce further protective measures such as 'Stalking Protection Orders'.

I interviewed Niki again in November 2022, to hear the continuation of her story. Despite her psychogenic stammer, which was brought on by the psychological abuse that she has endured, she was keen to share her frustrations regarding her experience of the legal process so far in her fight for justice.

'Mine is the very first serious case review where the victim has lived.'

It is ss..still going on. I have had to ring the police twice since he was ss..sentenced. It is just a joke! He got a four-month suspended sentence. He did a last-minute plea bargain to change the charge to 'harassment', which meant it was the earliest time that he could enter a plea, so they gave him a lighter ss..sentence with a two-month reduction. The restraining order that they issued is apparently just a bog ss..standard one that ss..states 'no direct or indirect contact'.

At the ss..sentencing hearing, he said that I had mentioned him on social media. I only have my FF…Facebook page and I have never mentioned his name. I know that I have never done anything illegal. I have not even said what has happened at all, ss..so someone we both know must have reported information back to him. I rang the police as somebody is putting mm..me at risk. The police told me that they cannot question my ex about this issue, as there has been no contact with me, therefore it is not a breach of the restraining order. So I said, hang on a minute, ss..so this guy has been allegedly ss..stalking me, and there is a ss..stalking hearing in FF..February to protect any future members of the public and also me but you can't ask him about it? Or, even give mm..me any words of advice? The police then told me that they could not give mm..me 'words of advice' anymore because of my case.

I messaged a couple of my ff..friends on FF..Facebook that I know are mutual friends of ours, to try to ff..find out if they had heard anything, but then my manipulative ex-partner reported me to the police for harassment. My mm..messages were in no way harassing.

To this day, the social care workers in my case ss..still haven't heard the full ss..story about what has really happened. Recently a ss..social worker told me that to help explain the ss..situation to the children, they plan to tell my four children that 'their daddy keeps mm..messaging mummy'…(pause and a large intake of breath)…. and I ww..went… but that's not what has happened!

Interestingly, the life-long RR..Restraining Order, which has been issued to me, is quite rare. They told me that it is bog ss..standard to only have the words: *'no direct or indirect contact'* on the order, so I have now contacted the House of Commons about this. They told me that 'non-molestation' orders are often more comprehensive and prohibitive. They told me that they are now drafting ss..something to request that more comprehensive Restraining Orders are issued. This should go live next week.

The CPS wrote to me, and they said that stalking is a rr..relatively new law, and I thought, nn..no, it's nn…not. I have had to learn all these things myself. I know SPOs are new. (January 2020), but the ss..stalking charge has been established for some time. Victims are often given inconsistent and misleading information.

The CPS then said that the harassment charges sit at the same as the stalking prosecuting ss..sentencing guidelines, and my case sits at '1b' culpability comfortably, and potentially it may sit at a '1a offence'.

I have had a different Prosecutor each time I went to court. One, who I did not even know, ww..walked into the court, and she said to me: *"It is going to be done today. That's it …end of."* I ss..said: *"Who are you? You are not the person I ss..saw last time"* (nervous laughter). The hearing was listed for 2 pm, and at 2:30 pm, she was ss..still under the impression that I would be rr..reading out my own impact statement (Victim Personal Statement) in court. I had to explain to her that I have a psychogenic ss..stammer and that there would be no way that I would be able to rr..read out a 15-page ss..statement. By the time I have read 10 pages I would probably pass out! She then handed it to mm..me, and told me to just read five lines, and that was all that ww..was read. They said that they ww..were not prepared to read out the whole impact statement. They only wanted to rr..read the ff..five lines that related to my mm..mental health. Apparently, it was sent to the Judge and it was rr..read later, but not during the hearing.

Two days bb..before the trial, my perpetrator did a plea bargain to enter **'Harassment Section 4'.** (*This is a common tactic by defence*) He pleaded guilty, but only to a mm..much lesser charge of **'Harassment, Section 4'.** When it came to the trial day, they said that he had pleaded guilty, and pre-sentence reports believe all options are open for committal. They even said that with the ss..seriousness of the offence, it should be a matter for the Crown Court, but at the ss..sentencing hearing that followed in a magistrates court, a totally different prosecutor just said: *"4 months suspended sentence".* I was shocked. I went: what! This is not ok!!

I have appealed to the Attorney General's Office, but because it was a ss..sentence that was passed in a MM..Magistrates Court, (where people off the street are able to make the decisions). Anyone can just apply to become a MM..Magistrate.

As my case was not heard in the Crown Court, the Attorney General's Office cannot appeal against the ss..sentence being unduly lenient. Ss..so I have had to now make a ff..further complaint to the Crown Prosecution Service (CPS). My case should have gone to the Crown Court List.

They used all the mm..mitigating factors, but no aggravating ff..factors were fought for, and my ex-partner committed every single one. The CPS has now finally admitted that this case should have gone to Crown Court, and they have now agreed to look at the ss..sentence being an unduly lenient sentence. They ss..say I will get an answer from them later this month, November 2022.

The probation officers only have information about my ex from the things that he ss..says to them. He is a real ss..smooth talker, and he has the gift of the gab. He comes across as vv..very charming and believable. He told the social worker that he had tracked down and worked out which school the children were now attending, and mistakenly the ss..social worker gave him the name of the school!

Lying and being deceitful is ww..what stalkers are very practised at, but it seems that the team in my case are totally oblivious to the devious tactics of a ss..stalker.

I was horrified when the children's ss..services mistakenly divulged information about where I was living and gave the location of the new ss..school that the children were attending. This breach was reported in the local newspaper, but my ex was not named. So I decided to remove mm..my own anonymity, and I gave my own ss..story to the press and on ss..social media. I was happy to go public about this. However, social services then asked me to make an undertaking in the ff. family court to not post anything on social media. That is like asking an abused victim to be quiet! I decided that I was not having it! The matter did go to the court, but they did not get their 'gag' order, as criminal proceedings are public under open justice.

My ex-husband doesn't know where I am living now, but apparently, he has a right to know where our children go to school. I am now living in a new secret location, and I have been advised that it will be unsafe for mm..me to go back to my home. They have offered me web cameras, and CCTV and security, but what they do not realise is that my mm..main concern is the psychological abuse. How is CCTV going to help? I am now on the emergency housing list to be rehomed. If you have children together with an abuser, you are pretty much ss..screwed. He is allowed unsupervised contact with the children and there is nn..nothing I can do about that.

In February this year, 2022, when my ex-partner came to my house to see the children, he removed the ss..speakers out my 'Alexas', so that when someone would dial in, it would not make a noise and therefore not be detected. My mum noticed something odd about the 'Alexas' when she was ss..staying at my house, and also a mutual friend confirmed to me that my ex had taken the speakers, but he was too ff..fearful of my ex-husband to come forward to inform the police and be a witness for mm..me. However, this action will not be able to be taken into consideration in my case, as it was not reported within the correct time, and it is now too late, as it happened over 6 months ago. FF..Friends who have witnessed his behaviour would like to ss..support me, but they know my ex, and they are also too ss..scared to come forward as witnesses, as they are ww..worried about him reacting badly towards them. He lives in the same community as them, and there is no ww..witness protection ss.scheme.

My ex-partner has also been intimidating towards other ff..friends of mine ww..when he has seen them in public places and this was just because they were acting on my behalf as a ww..witness. Apparently, though, these acts of intimidation which took place in public places, are not considered a criminal offence.

I ff..fell over and broke my nose so I had to delay a ff..family law session. My ex, who also self-represents himself for ff..family law, wrote a letter via the court to say: *'I advise your client to rearrange her surgery as it does not sound life-threatening.'* To mm..me, this is indirect contact and contravenes the Restraining Order, but because it was effectively considered contact from a solicitor, it was allowed. This is abuse. It is not ok!

My IDVA (Independent Violence Advisor) is very ss..supportive. She told me that she has never ss..seen a case like mm..mine. The social workers on my case are a little bit bitter at the moment, as they have egg on their face due to the breach that was made.

The four children I have with my ex-partner are open for family law. In domestic abuse, stalking and harassment cases the children are not protected under the social care guidelines. The onus is very much on the vv..victim to protect the care of the children. My ex is allowed unsupervised contact with the ff..four children that we have together. There is nn..nothing that I can do about this. Now that he has been convicted, he can do **Words & Pictures - signs of safety' (1)** - with our children totally unsupervised. This really concerns mm..me as my ex can then actually deny everything. I ff..feel that it is better done when he is supervised, as I know that he can lie.

The *'Words & Pictures'* programme is designed to help children to understand why they can't talk openly about their mm..mummy or daddy regarding certain things. I did it mm..myself with the children, but I got 'hh..hammered' by the social worker for doing so.

I ss..showed social services video footage of what my ex was doing with one of my children. They told me that the videos in question had already been investigated by the police and therefore they were not going to do anything more about it. But I insisted that what he had done was not ok. I was mortified by what I saw on the videos that I ff..found. I ss..showed the authorities the 11 videos I had showing his bb..behaviour, but they didn't care. In the videos, it clearly is his voice, but ss..still they don't seem to care.

My ex-husband remotely ww..wiped my iPhone when he was vv..voluntarily arrested. However, I re-logged into my 'iCloud' account and I managed to rr..reload my phone, and this is when I found these very distressing vv..videos of him harming and bullying the children. He also physically vaginally examined our daughter when she was 12, as supposedly she had thrush, but apparently, ss..social ss..services also consider this ok? Rr..really? They say it is not a criminal offence to do what he did, and they ss..said that it is acceptable if he is examining his daughter for health reasons. I am a midwife, and I have never vaginally examined a patient who has thrush!

My ex-partner's lawyer contested the application for a Stalking Protection Order, therefore the mm..magistrate would not agree to the police applying for an SPO in mm..my case. The mm..magistrate stated that the existing Restraining Order is enough. I am ff..furious and I am out to cause a ss..storm. Mine is the very first ss..serious case review where the victim has lived. My ss..stalking hearing is now planned to take place in February 2023.

The majority of victims in cases like mm..mine do not even contact the police and even if they do, often not mm..much is done. This is mostly because of a lack of training in this area. When a vv..victim does ask for help, it should be investigated further through the multi agencies that have received the specialist training. However, domestic abuse is not always vv..visible, and many victims will ss..suffer in ss..silence with no one to turn to. Psychological and emotional harm becomes an acceptable behaviour to vv..victims because they know little else. Like mm..myself, a victim can be ff..falsely accused of acquiescence. The police need to understand that vv..victims are not acquiescing, they are unknowingly being mm..moulded to comply with the perpetrator's ww..wishes, whilst also being deliberately alienated from their ff..friends and ff..family. Observers can often see tt..this happening but they feel helpless to ss..step in and become involved until the victim finally asks for help.

(1) Stalking Protection Orders:
https://www.cps.gov.uk/legal-guidelines/stalking-protection-orders

(2) How to Guide: Words & Pictures:
https://www.cescp.org.uk/pdf/signs-of-safety/how-to-guide-words-and-pictures.pdf

(3) VPS - Victim Personal Statement:
https://www.gov.uk/government/publications/victim-personal-statement

EXAMPLE OF A VICTIM PERSONAL STATEMENT

Writing a **VPS – Victim Personal Statement (3)** gives the victim the opportunity to have a voice in the criminal justice process. It allows the court to be more informed about the victim's life and to gain a broader understanding of how the crime has affected them. It provides an opportunity for the victim to communicate verbally, and/or in writing about how the abuse has and may still be continuing to impact them and their family. This can include physical, emotional, psychological, financial, or any other challenges that the victim and her family have suffered as a consequence of the perpetrator's actions.

Ideally, the statement should be kept as short and as succinct as possible, and clearly express the negative impact on the victim. As most victims are at their most traumatised prior to going to court, writing such a statement can be emotionally challenging and difficult to put together, particularly for someone who may not have the literary capabilities to express themselves through writing. I truly believe that all victims should be provided with professional support and given advice on how to put together such a statement.

Niki was denied her opportunity to have her voice heard, as due to her psychogenic stammer she was not able to read her complete VPS during the court proceedings, (probably due to the length of the document and the allocated court time). With her full agreement, I have included a section from her Victim Personal Statement in this book, so at least her feelings can be openly expressed, and she is able to finally relay how the stalking and abuse have impacted her life. (Names and sensitive information have been removed).

NIKI'S PERSONAL STATEMENT

I fear for my life because of the defendant's long history of coercive and controlling abuse, and the recent relentless stalking behaviour that he has undertaken following the end of our relationship.

My children and I have endured harm and stress for many years. They have witnessed many frightening and inappropriate events that they should not have had to experience. They have also suffered direct coercive behaviour from the defendant as he has tried to get them to provide him with information so that he can target me further. The incidents that took place between February 2020 and June 2020 and the incidents that occurred following these dates have been very damaging to my children and myself. This has resulted in a rapid deterioration of my own personal mental and physical health, has had a significant impact on my independence, my career, and my ability to sustain a normal lifestyle for myself and my children.

I suffer from recurrences and horrific nightmares for which I must take medication to aid my sleep. Sometimes the flashbacks can happen during the day and can involve a stranger in the public turning around to me; and in that instant, I can physically see the defendant's face in the place of someone else. This causes me excessive amounts of stress and has resulted in agoraphobia. I am unable to leave the house and attend my place of work or education due to this severe agoraphobia. I feel unsafe, and I have a constant sense of hyper-vigilance. In my head, I can still hear myself begging the police and the children's services that someone must do something to help me. His behaviour is turning from obsessive to the point where, if he can't have me then nobody else can. I honestly think that he will go as far as setting fire to the house with us in it.

Every time that I receive an innocent anonymous parcel from a friend I immediately panic, thinking it is yet another unwanted gift from him. I dare not go to work or my place of education following the malicious email with false allegations that he sent to my employer when he imitated being a doctor. The fact that I had to turn to my work colleagues for help, now means that everyone at work knows about my situation and now I fear that they may deem me as unable to work effectively. As a protector of vulnerable people, I find it devastating and disempowering to be thought of as a vulnerable person. I was once a brave, strong, empowering individual who protected others.

The manipulating behaviour of the defendant even fooled the local police. Following the defendant's stroke in May 2020, the police were led to believe that the defendant was house bound. Without informing me and following his house move to the next street to me, the police removed the bail conditions that were there to protect me as the police said they were satisfied that he would not continue to be a threat to me due to his mobility issues. This was later found not to be the case, as he continued to deliberately pass through my street. When the defendant moved into the next street from where we lived, he utilised the fact that he was still on the tenancy at our previous address, as having a 'legal right' to the premises. I could not leave the house safely due to him living in such close to me. This meant that I had to regularly change my route to school and to work, and I became obsessed with securing my home.

The defendant abused his use of parental responsibility to gain sensitive information about me and my life through the school and other services. He started involving other people to report my movements, and he was asking probing questions of my older children. His proximity and the local connections he had with the acquaintances in the local shop meant that I had no choice but to move out of the area.

The defendant was advised by the police to not contact me. This made me feel a bit better as I thought that his harassment might stop, but it didn't, and my life then became unbearable. Now that he was not able to instigate actions directly towards me, he moved onto a campaign against my friends and loved ones, making false allegations. I felt guilty that my friends and my family were also suffering and being targeted by him. Just because of me. I felt that this was my fault and I felt so isolated. Due to his false allegations, my mother came under investigation at her place of work, and my father was also maliciously accused of theft of items from my property, which did not exist or were already in the defendant's possession.

I applied for a Non-Molestation Order, which was awarded. However, the defendant then caused me further stress by applying to have the Non-Molestation Order discharged. The order was very extensive due to the number of incidents that had occurred and the excessive behaviour that he had displayed over the short period of time. This order expired on June 24th, 2021. However, due to multiple loopholes within the order, it was still possible for him to inflict psychological trauma, such as posting passive Facebook posts, which were directed at me. These actions did not breach the Non-Molestation Order as the posts only referred to me, and he did not directly name me.

When the defendant was forbidden from approaching me directly, he then started a cruel online campaign through social media, which lead to members of the local community becoming aware of certain false allegations against me. I had no other option than to flee the area, but at this point, the defendant then used the family court's parental responsibility to try to obstruct this house move. He used a prohibited steps order to ensure that if I did move, then the new location would be known to him. Fortunately, after many stressful and traumatic months, my move was granted, however, this was financially debilitating for me. Once I had successfully moved away, children's services put my life in danger by leaking the whereabouts of my new location to the defendant. This is when I thought that the only way that the truth would be known, and I could finally make it all stop, would be to end my own life. I am still plagued by recurring thoughts of self-harm and suicide.

I am writing this impact statement to show the real devastating impact that the defendant's violent and abusive behaviour has had on myself and my children. The damage that he has caused me is life changing. I now struggle to verbally communicate due to my stammer, which has been caused by the psychological trauma. I must take multiple medications daily to regulate my speech and to sustain my normal daily activities such as grocery shopping and cooking meals. I have received specialist input from multiple services including social workers, my GP, adult social care, the local hospital, CRISIS team, Night Café, and Bric. I am currently awaiting the allocation of a Community Psychiatric Nurse to help me with the agoraphobia, suicidal thoughts, anxiety, tremors, pathogenic stammer, multiple panic attacks, insomnia, and parasomnia.

I truly believe that the defendant will not stop harassing me until I am dead. I have always voiced, and I still voice that he will not stop his manipulative campaign against me until I stop breathing. I wish for him to never find me. I wish to be able to lead a normal daily life where I can feel safe and go to the park without feeling fear. Where I can escape the terrifying thoughts in my head and be able to look at the police and believe that they are there to protect me rather than having to associate them with the prolonged abuse that I have sustained.

I have lived in constant fear for two years and I don't feel that I will ever feel safe again. I used to be a strong confident individual who helped in the care of hundreds of other people and helped to save lives, but now I am too scared to set foot out of my own door. I am living like a prisoner who has no freedom and no escape.

*'Justice? You get justice in the next world;
in this world you have the law.'*

William Gaddis
(1994)

Being Believed

His violent acts have changed my life
My mind is not the same.
How could he do these things to me?
My body feels the shame.
It still remembers everything
And my mind remembers more.
The trauma takes its toll on me
So please believe my words.

I sense that you think otherwise.
My distress is hard to fathom.
I used to be a fearless woman
Full of laughter, fun, and joy.
But now I feel so vulnerable,
Timid, fearful, and coy.
The pain and hurt block off my mind
So please believe my words.

I want to forget that awful day
And return to times before.
But the journey seems impossible,
I cannot find the door.
Pull yourself together girl
Self-pity is not your style.
Although I try, it does not work.
So please believe my words.

I want this to end and be forgotten.
Erasing images of the past.
The future must be there somewhere
But I am not sure what it holds.
It is hard to think of anything else
Except the violence I endured.
It will help me heal if you do believe
So please believe my words.

Melissa Stockdale
(2020)

4

ANNE

Rebecca – 'My Merry Sunshine'

(Interviewed April 2022)

In memory of Rebecca Rice 1988 - 2006

Introducton to Anne

I first met Anne by chance whilst I was sitting on a wooden memorial bench that is situated in a local area of woodland. I had been walking my dog and I sat down for a while on the bench under the trees. As I was sitting down enjoying the natural surroundings and the peace and quiet, I read the words that were carved out on the bench. I wondered who Rebecca might be. Her name was inscribed on the back of the seat and I could see that she was born in 1988, the same year as my own daughter, but I could see that she had only lived until 2006.

As I was reflecting on what may have happened to this young girl, a lady walked towards me through the trees with her dogs. She sat down next to me on the bench and introduced herself as Anne and we chatted. This was when Anne informed me that she was the person who had asked a local craftsman to build the bench that we were both sitting on. She had it placed there in memory of her daughter Rebecca, who had been brutally murdered in 2006.

Anne told me that she had recently been contacted by the prison service to say that her daughter's killer could be soon released from prison. Anne was devastated to hear this. In 2007, he had pleaded guilty to her daughter's murder and he was given a life sentence with an order to serve a minimum term of 16 years in prison. However, Anne felt that it was wrong that his life sentence for her daughter's murder was less than the 18 years that Rebecca had been alive. Anne was struggling to come to terms with his possible release.

I visited Anne's home in April 2022 to listen to her full story. When I arrived, Anne introduced me to her daughter's horse which was grazing in the paddock with two other horses. Anne still cares for the horses, but she does not ride anymore, following her injuries caused by a riding accident in 2020. Anne suffered serious head and spinal injuries caused by the fall, and these will have life-long effects on her physical and mental health. Anne revealed to me that in her darkest moments, she sometimes wishes that she had not survived the fall.

Anne showed me photos of her beautiful daughter, Rebecca, and gave me a collection of newspaper cuttings with stories and reports of Rebecca's murder. Anne also shared with me a poignant letter that she had written many years later after the tragic loss of her daughter. Here are the words that Anne wrote:

'Rebecca – My Merry Sunshine'

Sixteen years ago, my daughter Rebecca was murdered. She was left to die bleeding to death from multiple stab wounds in a flat on her own. The last time I saw Rebecca was on the Friday night, leaving my house with 'him' (her partner). I was never going to see her again alive.

My husband (now ex-husband) and I tried to contact her on the next day, Saturday, to no avail. We walked to her flat on the Saturday evening to see if she was there. The curtains were closed, and her car had gone. We did not know what to think.

On the Sunday morning, my husband reported to the local police, that Rebecca and her partner were both missing. The police told us to stay put and they would investigate. However, we were very concerned so after a while, we went to her flat. When we arrived there, we saw the police outside her property.

There was yellow and black tape all around the front door. The police then told us that there was a female body inside. It was then that my whole world collapsed, and my life ended. I instantly ran away like a wounded animal in so much pain and fear. I ran towards the road and then just stopped and sat on the kerb. I often wonder now, why I just did not run into the road.

If ever I see black and yellow police tape now, I feel those same feelings all over again as it takes me straight back to that awful day.

A very kind police constable took my husband and myself home, and he stayed with us until the **'FLO' (Family liaison Officer – a police officer who is specially trained to work with bereaved families)** *arrived. That police constable who helped us, has since died of cancer. Life is so cruel.*

So, sixteen years later, how am I? My heart is broken. Time does not heal. I think of Rebecca every hour of every day and I try to blot out how she died, but I will never come to terms with the fact that she died alone after suffering such horrific injuries. This will always haunt me. Mums should be there to protect their children.

I do not live. I just exist. I go through the daily motions of living. I get up, do some jobs, take the dogs for a walk. Every day is the same. Friends just melt away.

I have five grandchildren who have never been able to meet their Auntie Rebecca. They know about her, as my two sons make sure of that. They have not been told how she died yet, but when they are older, they will be told. As a family, we try to protect their innocence as long as possible.

I often ask myself: 'Would Rebecca have had her own children now, if she had lived?' I have been denied her children as she has. Rebecca and I shared a love of horses and I wonder if we would have now been teaching her children to ride. Living holds so many dreams, but now these have been destroyed.

It really is too painful to continue writing this. I have a life sentence, which will only end when I eventually die.

Soon after her daughter's death, Anne wrote a **VPS (Victim Personal Statement)** to explain in her own words how the murder of Rebecca had affected her life. This was supposed to be read out during the court proceedings. Anne was distraught when this was not shared with the court as expected, so she decided to contact her local newspaper to have her personal statement published. Being able to publicly share her deep feelings regarding her daughter's murder, was a vital part of aiding Anne's emotional recovery. The headline in the local paper quoted Anne as saying:

'The thought of Rebecca suffering immeasurable pain and experiencing fear whilst being stabbed by this monster horrifies me. Yes, I am broken by this act of barbarity.'

(Bulstrode, M., 2007, February 24)

ANNE

'Sixteen years for him - but a Life Sentence for me'

(Interviewed April 2022)

'Sixteen years for him - but a Life Sentence for me'

I didn't like Rebecca's boyfriend when I first met him, but I didn't want to upset Rebecca, so I didn't say anything to her. He was 32 years old and she was only 17 at the time. The age difference worried her father and I. She met him when she was out with friends in the local town. He had the *'talk'* and he could be very charming. He drove a Porsche, which wasn't his, but my daughter thought it was. I tried to do my best for my daughter so I made him feel welcome here, even though I did not really like him. I just thought the relationship would run its course.

On that fateful Friday, Rebecca and I went out riding together in the afternoon and we chatted. Rebecca talked to me about leaving him. I thought to myself: *'Good, she is going to leave him.'* I was treading on eggshells and I did not want to say too much to her. I do remember though that while we were unsaddling the horses, I said to her: *"Rebecca, you will always have a home here, always,* (pause) *always."*

On reflection, I could have done loads more to help Rebecca, but I didn't know then how bad things were between them. I thought that when she told him that it was over, that would be the end of it.

Rebecca had dated him for a while, but that Friday, I remember she said to me: *"Mum, I can't live like this."* It was clear that she wanted to end the relationship. I was about to leave for a holiday in Canada, so I told my daughter that I would help her to sort things out when I returned from my trip to Canada, but he murdered her that night.

Just hours before he murdered her, they were both having tea with me, right here in this house. This was after my daughter and I had driven to pick him up from the train station earlier in the evening.

I found out from friends that Rebecca would sometimes go out to the pub with her girlfriends and that he would follow her there, and then he would lurk around and wait outside for an hour or so while she was inside. He was very…what is the word that I am looking for (pause) 'controlling?' I don't know, I can't think anymore. Horrible man, I hate him. I loathe him.

Rebecca's partner stabbed her ten times on the front and the back of her body that night. One of the wounds was 12 cm deep, piercing her liver, and experts had said that she would have remained conscious while these injuries were being inflicted. After the vicious attack, her partner left her there alone to die, and he drove off in her car, taking Rebecca's mobile phone with him and then disposing of it. So, Rebecca would have been unable to call for help even if she had been conscious.

He called the police two days later, on the Sunday to confess to the murder after he had been persuaded to do so by his brother. When the police arrived to arrest him, they found a length of rope tied with a slipknot, and they saw that he had tried to slit his wrists. However, when he was questioned later, he created a story to the police that Rebecca had attacked him first, by stabbing him in the chest with a knife.

The judge dismissed the perpetrator's story completely, and when sentencing him for Rebecca's murder, he said:

"This was a frenzied attack, in which you were completely out of control. You left that girl still conscious and bleeding to death on the floor in the kitchen."

I will never forget that Monday after the murder when we had to go with the police to the hospital to formally identify her. She did not look like Rebecca. I looked at her hands, then I said: *"Oh yes, they are her hands."* Rebecca had beautiful hands (pause). It was awful. My son came with us too.

The police in Canada then went looking for my other son who was abroad travelling. They went to the youth hostel where he was staying and they left a message at the reception there. When my son came back to the hostel, the receptionist told him that the police were looking for him. Initially, he thought it was a joke. He went to the police station and he asked them: *"Is it my mum and dad?"* It was then that the police told him that his sister had passed away.

The police got my son on a flight back to England – I don't know how they did that. My husband and I drove to Heathrow to pick him up. The police escorted us there, and they provided us with a room on our own to talk to our son.

Both my sons were devastated. Rebecca's funeral was not until six weeks later as they had to do a post-mortem on her body in Norwich. The solicitor requested this. The police assured me that they would travel to Norwich and be there with Rebecca's body. Someone at the court released her body as soon as they could, and then we were able to have the funeral.

Suffolk police even came to support us at Rebecca's funeral. She had a horse-drawn carriage to carry her to the church, and the police detective even stood out in the road and stopped the traffic so the carriage could pass through. They were fantastic.

After the funeral, the police told us things about the man who murdered our daughter. He had a history of drug dealing, and he was apparently engaged to a girl before he began dating Rebecca, and they also informed us that he had once attempted to strangle his fiancé. This was done in front of his parents!

Rebecca purchased a horsebox, and I remember the day that he brought the horsebox over to my house here to park the box in the yard next to the stables. When I looked inside the cab of the horsebox, I found something under the driver's seat. It was a wedding album. Inside it, there were photographs of him with his wife! He was married! I was shocked (pause). He was married!

The police told me that they had interviewed his wife. Apparently, she told the police that he had left her after just a few months after being married. He was totally crazy, and poor Rebecca was so young and vulnerable, very vulnerable, (pause) yeah, very vulnerable (quiet pause).

The police told us that he had pleaded guilty to killing Rebecca, and the court hearing was planned for the next day. I took time off work to attend court, but when we got to court the judge said that he had received a letter from the perpetrator the night before declaring that he was innocent. As he had initially pleaded guilty, the judge was dismissive of him now changing his mind, and a time was set for another court hearing.

Once we were sat in the court he changed his plea again, and he pleaded guilty. He was given a life prison sentence. I took one of my healing crystals with me to court. I was so angry that this man had taken my daughter's life. I just wanted to throw the crystal at him.

We gave character references and our personal statements to the judge, but he never read them out aloud in the court as we expected he would. The judge did not even look at us. It was so upsetting for us all.

My husband and I both decided that as it was such a horrific killing, people should know what really happened. This is why we contacted the press. Here are the newspaper cuttings and a letter that I wrote, (Anne hands me the newspaper cuttings and a letter for me to read). The newspaper printed our personal statements that we had prepared for the court hearing. We just wanted our story to be told.

I don't want him in Suffolk. I don't want him here. I am worried that when he is released, he could just turn up. (Anne begins to cry) I'm sorry, I'm sorry (long pause).

Apparently, it is recorded in the police notes, but I hope they get an order to prevent him from being in Suffolk… I don't want him near me.

There was one point when they told me that he was soon going to be released from prison and could be transferred to an open prison. I told them that he could not be in the open prison in Suffolk. I remember them saying to me: *"Why not?"* I was so angry. I live alone now. He knows where I am. What is to stop him just turning up? I just don't trust him. I could go to the churchyard to visit Rebecca's grave and even find him there.

I lose track of time now, and I get muddled with the years, maybe this is because I was unconscious for several months after my accident.

I have not heard anything about him for a while now. I don't feel any differently now as I did then. The organisation **SAMM (an agency that offers Support After Murder and Manslaughter (1)** were also very helpful and they send me things like this every two years. (Anne shows me the supportive letters and correspondence from **SAMM**).

I went back to supply teaching after my daughter's murder, but I could not continue. I got divorced six or seven years ago. I was married for 34 years. I don't go out now. I walk my dogs and I do my horse duties. I don't have friends anymore. Well, I did have one friend, but I haven't seen her for a year and a half.

When I finally came out of hospital after the fall from my horse, people did not seem to want to have anything to do with me. I used to meet friends when I walked my dogs on the heath, but I don't even see them anymore. I was in hospital in June. The 7th June is when the accident happened. A friend did visit me in the hospital once. I don't know what I have done to upset them. It is a horrid thing to say, but sometimes, I wish that I had not survived that fall from my horse.

I like to go walking in the forest as then I do at least get to chat to other people who are out walking their dogs. I often sit on the bench that I had put there in memory of Rebecca. There used to be an old cottage situated in that pretty place apparently. Hence all the daffodils that are planted there. I love sitting there.

I have had messages from spiritualists to say that Rebecca is ok in the spirit world, and this is very comforting to hear. Sometimes I have wonderful dreams about my daughter in heaven. They are lovely. I try to meditate when I can, as this helps. Spiritualism is very important for me. I am getting there, but my life now is just looking after my five animals, and seeing my grandchildren. I feel that Rebecca is here with me in spirit all the time.

Once, some years ago, when I went to the church to place flowers on Rebecca's grave, I met a couple who were there sitting on the bench adjacent to her grave. The man talked to me, while his wife, Irma listened. Soon after this meeting, I received this beautiful poem from Irma. It came in the post. (Anne passes me a copy of the poem). Irma had somehow managed to find my address, and she kindly sent me this poem that she had written for me. Her words still offer me great comfort.

(1) SAMM – Support After Murder & Manslaughter: https://samm.org.uk

Rebecca in May

I waited for her to come
I watch her come in through the iron gate.
Young and purposeful is her walk.
In my heart, I know the stranger I never met
"Come and sit on the bench," she said.
I watch her not daring to raise my eyes
Or listen to her thoughts.

She made your dress pretty today
She picked and brushed the colours
In her tenderness, you are no more than five
As she brushes your hair lovingly while you sleep
In the changing seasons and this landscape now
The years will not corrupt the innocence of your youth.

The bench holds time and the memories
Carved so the wood will outlast 18 falls of cherry
blossoms
And the traveller who pauses from the wet footpaths
From criss-crossing the mean cuts of farmers
May see beyond the changing greens of barley fields
The yellowing of late spring matches the gold in your hair.

The rains came last night
Still, she brings water for your hair.

Without a word
She walks older and slower through the iron gate.

Irma Upex-Huggins
- Poet and Activist for Women's Issues
(2009)

Conclusion

According to the Office for National Statistics (ONS) in 2020, police in England and Wales recorded more than 80,000 incidents of stalking although they estimate that 2.5 million people every year experience stalking. The National Police Chiefs Council (NPCC) found stalking crimes rose by 18,000 in the period between 2018 and 2022, however, the National Stalking Consortium confirm that only 5% of stalking cases in England and Wales result in a charge by the Crown Prosecution Service (CPS).

- **1 in 3 women and 1 in 4 men have experienced some form of physical violence by an intimate partner.**

- **An intimate partner has injured 1 in 7 women and 1 in 25 men.**

- **1 in 6 women and 1 in 17 men have experienced stalking.**

- **Every 4 days a partner or ex-partner kills a woman.**

All the victims who shared their personal stories for this publication expressed to me that they wished that they had listened more carefully to their own gut instincts during the formation of their relationships. Several of them mentioned little niggles or certain odd behaviours that they had noticed in the early stages, which they would now recognise as **'red flags'** and wish that they had sought help sooner.

If you find yourself in a situation where you are receiving non-stop phone calls, text messages, emails, and/or persistent unwanted attention from someone who is making you feel uncomfortable and vulnerable, you can contact The Suzy Lamplugh Trust for helpful advice regarding stalking. On their website, there is also an online self-assessment tool (written in multiple languages) that will inform you about the different types of behaviour and strategies that stalkers may use. You will be able to detect whether your personal experiences are deemed as stalking, and the information could help to mitigate risks to your own personal safety. This can be accessed at:
https://amibeingstalked.suzylamplugh.org

Leeway Domestic Violence and Abuse Services https://www.leewaysupport.org also offer free and confidential support.

'Enter new relationships with your eyes wide open.
Like the rest of us, most psychopathic con artists
and love thieves initially hide their dark side
by putting their best foot forward.'

Robert D. Hare
(*Without Conscience*, 1993, p 211)

Being Aware

Obviously, the best scenario for anyone who finds themselves in an abusive situation would be to immediately curtail the relationship as soon as they recognise the pattern of coercive or controlling behaviour. However, this is not always possible as they may be totally financially dependent on the abuser, have children together, or be involved with someone who exhibits such extreme behaviour to suggest a dark triad of personality, of *'Narcissism, Machiavellianism, and Psychopathy'*, (Paulhus & Williams, 2002).

Such individuals as these (narcissists, con artists, and psychopaths) will be exceptionally adept at presenting only positive behaviour, and they will come across as utterly charming and charismatic as their intent is to manipulate and convince their prey into committing to them. They will display complete indifference to the callous violence they inflict on their victim, and show zero regret. Indeed, often their visible reaction after being abusive or threatening may signal pure pleasure, and/or smug satisfaction for any damage they have inflicted. This cruelty, meanness, and their cold-blooded, sadistic enjoyment of inflicting pain and causing suffering is terrifying for the victim to witness.

Many sociopaths and psychopaths are prone to pathological lying and their lack of conscience makes lying a guilt-free activity for them. They often behave in immoral or illegal ways with a complete disregard for rules and laws.

How does someone spot patterns of such behaviour? The survivors of stalking and abuse who contributed their stories to this book admitted that they had made several mistakes during their relationships. In hindsight, they regret that they did not act upon these things sooner.

- Not listening to their gut instinct.

- Ignoring the early warning signs or 'red flags' and not recognising the abuse earlier.

- Not taking adequate personal safety precautions.

- Neglecting to ask more pertinent questions at the commencement of their relationship.

- Divulging too much sensitive and private information about themselves to their new partner.

- Not giving a clear message to express that they are not interested in pursuing a relationship.

- Being manipulated and easily taken in by the charm and the persuasive 'talk' of the perpetrator.

- Not taking the threats or the violence directed towards them seriously or giving enough thought to the potential consequences.

- Not realising that it is impossible to discuss or reason logically with a stalker or abuser.

- Not informing family, friends or work colleagues earlier about their concerns.

- Failing to seek professional help sooner from relevant agencies or police.

- Blaming themselves for the situation they are in.

- Ignoring their own personal needs and their psychological well-being during and after the abuse.

- Having the courage to leave and/or report the crime earlier.

While listening to the survivor's stories, it soon became apparent that a common behaviour trait of the abusers in each case was to have a complete lack of an emotional response, or ability to show any genuine concern about the overall welfare of their partners. All the perpetrators discussed in this book showed a distinct indifference towards their partner's physical and mental health, and some offenders would even deliberately abandon their partner completely during times of illness or pain.

It could be considered in some cases, that the perpetrators seemed to enjoy inflicting pain and discomfort. **'Duper's delight'** is a term that is often used for this type of behaviour, and it is when a successful fraud or liar becomes delighted and enthralled by his or her accomplishment. 'Duper's delight' can be seen as a micro expression, which is normally an inappropriate flashing smile.

I will never forget witnessing the huge grimacing smile on my partner's face during his violent assault on me. He behaved like an over-excited child, staring at me intensely with black vacant eyes. He laughed out loud with utter delight as he witnessed the devastating effect his actions were having on me. He saw the absolute fear showing on my face, and this gave him an exhilarating thrill. This kind of grimacing smile or odd facial reaction shows that the person is finding pure pleasure in the way that they have managed to manipulate someone. It demonstrates a rush of pride and a sense of power that they believe they have over another person.

Behaviour Traits and Warning Signs

After sharing their stories, I asked each participant to complete a checklist that I had prepared, which listed various behaviours that their partners may have displayed during their abusive relationship. The most common behaviour traits observed by them were as follows:

- **Initially charming, charismatic, likeable, funny and entertaining -** will use 'love bombing' techniques to fast-track the relationship. This 'honeymoon' period often lasts less than one year.

- **Impulsive and grandiose with an inflated ego.**

- **Selfish and arrogant -** often irresponsible and erratic.

- **Would use derogatory terms to describe their previous partner -** often using words like 'neurotic', 'pathetic' or 'psychotic'.

- **Devious and deceitful** - capable of telling multiple lies, and able to create believable elaborate stories.

- **Being highly critical of their partner's family and friends -** will often use lies or be patronising and insulting about people close to you to persuade you to completely detach from them.

- **Uses threatening behaviour** - will use sensitive personal information that has been privately shared to gain control and cause more harm and distress.

- **Uses 'gaslighting' techniques** - to cause uneasiness and doubt.

- **Manipulative and intimidating.**

- **Moody and attention-seeking.**

- **Lack of empathy** - completely indifferent to their partner's physical and emotional wellbeing.

- **Very persuasive, dominant and controlling.**

- **Jealous and possessive.**

- **Displays a sense of entitlement.**

- **Capable of physical violence and psychological abuse.**

- **Enjoys instilling fear -** through emotional abuse or by using implied verbal threats and physical violence.

- **Experiences money problems, and/or debt issues.**

- **Parasitic lifestyle.**

- **Demanding** -sexually, financially, emotionally, and of their partner's time.

- **Uses the children or pets to manipulate or cause fear, harm and distress.**

- **Uses the court system, police and public services to manipulate or delay legal proceedings to cause further harm and distress.**

- **Persistent.**

- **Obsessive.**

- **Will steal possessions** - when the relationship ends. They often vandalise the home or steal personal items and/or contents.

- **Causes criminal damage to their partner's vehicle, home or possessions.**

- **Stalking** - engages in some form of physical or psychological stalking or cyber-stalking tactics, to seek revenge, and have power and control.

It was noted that most victims tended to experience heightened aggression after confronting their partners and/or reporting their crimes. The behaviour of abusers who have been caught out should never be underestimated. They will go to extraordinary lengths to seek revenge and may also attempt to deliberately damage the reputation and lives of their victims.

As the stories in this book show, aggressors will often lie, manipulate the facts, tamper with evidence or even commit fraud to avoid being charged. Despite overwhelming evidence against them, they will continue to profess to the world that they are the innocent party.

The perpetrators may also use false defaming information to encourage other important parties to side with them. Sometimes the aggressor may put in counter allegations to the police to gain sympathy and claim that they are the 'victim'. All these deceitful actions are designed to redirect attention away from the crime that they are being charged with. They know that by creating fictitious charges, not only will this cause further harm and distress to the victim and create a significant delay to legal proceedings, but it will also throw the spotlight back onto the victim.

Strategies For Survival and Achieving Justice

Psychological abuse is always much harder to prove than physical abuse, therefore, it is important for any survivor to gather as much recorded evidence as possible to present to the police in an organised way, along with any witness statements to support their case.

If the victim can be proactive in this way and is willing to invest their own time and energy into building a solid case to help the police, then I truly believe that the survivor will also gain a sense of satisfaction and empowerment through playing a significant role in the process of bringing the perpetrator to justice.

To be able to bring appropriate charges against the perpetrator, the CPS (Crown Prosecution Service) require sufficient evidence that captures the patterns of abuse that have repeatedly occurred on at least two or more occasions. On the following page is an example of a form that could be used by victims of abuse to demonstrate to the police the types of behaviour that they are experiencing. These offences could be relevant for further investigation and assist in bringing the perpetrator to justice.

Rule of F.O.U.R

Fixated, **O**bsessive, **U**nwanted, **R**epeated behaviour.

Can you provide information about any fixated, obsessive, unwanted behaviour that has been exhibited towards you? If so, tick the appropriate box, then, in your own words define the behaviour in the box provided below, logging the location, dates, and the time, along with any witness details if possible. Share this evidence with the police when reporting the abuse.

Type of Behaviour	Yes	No
F - Fixated Behaviour		
O - Obsessive Behaviour		
U - Unwanted Behaviour		
R - Repeated Behaviour		

Coercive Control

In January 2022, in England and Wales, new laws were determined for ten forms of psychological abuse termed *'coercive control'* within a relationship. With this information in mind, I created a simple checklist as a helpful guide for victims experiencing such abuse. This checklist when completed by the victim could be used to guide them in the right direction for preparing the necessary evidence required to support the crimes that have been committed against them. Using this checklist will hopefully provide victims with more confidence to report such offences to the police.

Presenting a completed checklist and providing any related evidence in the form of an organised dated log sheet, which may include texts, letters, photos, screenshots, or videos. In addition, being able to provide the names of any witnesses who are willing to provide supportive statements to confirm that such crimes have been committed, along with detailed information on how this behaviour has affected the victim, will demonstrate to the police, and the CPS (Crown Prosecution Service), that the victim has seriously considered the abuse.

10 Signs of Coercive Control Within a Relationship

In England and Wales, the following ten acts towards a partner are considered illegal.

Tick the relevant boxes that may apply to you.

	Offence	Yes	No
1	**Forcing you to engage in sexual acts and/or sharing sexually explicit images of a partner:** The new laws surrounding 'Revenge Porn' make it illegal for someone to share intimate photographs of you with anyone, online or otherwise.		
2	**Economic Abuse:** Restricting access to finances, coerced debt, and/or controlling spending. Even if they earn more money than you, the law says your partner cannot stop you from accessing cash within the relationship.		
3	**Intentionally undermining the victim:** Putting you down, persistent name-calling, mocking and other forms of insulting behaviour. Forcing you to account for your time. Using 'gaslighting' techniques.		

4	**Acts of coercion:** Forcing or persuading you to do things that you are unwilling to do, isolating you from friends or family. Controlling and monitoring your access to social media and your devices. Blocking calls and intercepting emails. Telling you where you can or cannot go. Threatening to harm you or take away children and/or pets.		
5	**Emotional and psychological abuse:** Your partner might not physically assault you, but if they are doing enough to intentionally undermine or frighten you, they are committing an offence. This could include using their size to intimidate you or breaking things around the house. Suggesting verbally that your life is in danger.		
6	**Threats:** Repeated threats to reveal personal, private and sensitive information about you. This could include revealing details about your health, faith, religion or sexual orientation, and/or making false allegations about you to family, friends, work colleagues, and the wider community with the intention of deliberately stigmatizing you, or to deliberately cause harm and distress.		

7	**Use of Spyware:** Putting tracking devices on your phone or your car. It is now illegal under new legislation to monitor a person using online communication tools or spyware.		
8	**Extreme Jealousy:** Making persistent accusations of cheating. Deliberately preventing you from going to work or attending normal leisure activities. Refusing access to various ways for you to be able to communicate with others.		
9	**Exerting power and control:** Making and enforcing you to abide by stringent rules and regulations set by your partner. Dictating or restricting what you wear, when and where you eat, sleep, work or study, or whom you see or talk to. Preventing you from improving your education.		
10	**Reproductive coercion and sexual coercion:** including restricting a victim's access to birth control, and demanding sex. Also, forcing use of, or restricting access to alcohol or drugs. Denying access to medical care or prescribed medication. Using your health status, immigration status or religious beliefs to threaten you.		

Remember, any of these ten behaviours are not normal and they can lead to more violent actions and in some cases, murder.

The laws in the UK are being constantly reviewed and updated regarding physical violence, harassment, coercive control, domestic abuse, sexual assault, rape, and stalking.

Women's Aid were one of the staunch campaigners, alongside survivors and other activists to secure vital changes in the Domestic Abuse Act which was adopted on 29 April 2021. This Act strengthens the response across all agencies to provide further protection for all those people who experience domestic abuse and enhances measures in place to bring perpetrators to justice. As well as criminal justice reforms, it introduces important key changes to incorporate a legal definition of domestic abuse which now recognises children as victims and includes a provision for a Domestic Abuse Commissioner to stand up for survivors and provide life-saving domestic abuse services.

Councils have a legal duty to fund support for survivors to be in 'safe accommodation' and guarantee that all survivors will have a priority need for housing and be able to keep a secure tenancy in social housing if they need to escape an abuser.

Survivors benefit from new protections in the family and civil courts, including a ban on abusers from cross-examining their victims. Survivors are also guaranteed access to special measures which will include separate waiting rooms, alternative entrances and exits and use of screens in the court.

Doctors are also banned from charging for medical evidence of domestic abuse, including for legal aid, and the government has a duty to issue a code of practice on how data is shared between the public services that survivors might report to.

The Act also outlines new criminal offences to include post-separation coercive control, non-fatal strangulation, threats to disclose private sexual images and a ban on abusers using a defence of 'rough sex'.

Reporting a Crime

When reporting a crime that is being committed against you, ask a friend or a family member to go with you to the police station for support, and as a witness. Organise your evidence beforehand and keep copies of any documents/photos that you present to the police. Include copies of any previous convictions or court orders that relate to your situation. Keep a record of the names of the officers that you talk to and record any crime numbers. If you feel that your complaint is not being taken seriously, then request to speak to a senior officer.

On the following page is a form (with a sample entry) that could be used to keep a written record of any abuse and stalking events as they happen. It is important to include supportive evidence from any witnesses, along with their contact details and to include information about who it was reported to.

Presenting organised and collated information in this way will assist the course of prosecution, and it will encourage the authorities to proceed to court, confident in the knowledge that the victim of the crime is willing to push for charges, despite being traumatised and fearful of the perpetrator.

Be vigilant and proactive. Record and report every act committed against you and include as much detail as you can with supportive evidence and witness contact details.

Record of Abuse, Stalking Events and Witness Information

Date	Time	Event Details	Location	Witness	Reported To	Crime Number
6/3/24	8am	Husband followed me in his car to the station, got out of his car then grabbed me from behind and used threatening language to me at the train station while I was purchasing my ticket	Woking train station	Man in ticket office. John Smith 07799 912311	Local police by phone. Spoke to PC Rob Jones	CAS 123/524

Recently, there has been much public criticism of various police forces, and some of this is obviously warranted. However, I still believe that the victims/survivors need to have more faith in their own abilities, as they are the ones who have first-hand experience of the perpetrator, and their input and evidence are invaluable. If victims are granted easier access to the vital services available, given the emotional support that they require, and are provided with an insight into the relevant legal procedures that relate to the crimes that are being committed against them, it will then enable them to have more confidence to proactively engage in cooperating and assisting the police to progress their own case forward.

Often the survivor's perspective of events is dismissed and their feelings and views regarding the perpetrator are overlooked, ignored or side-lined with the emphasis being put on dealing with the perpetrator. When survivors first contact the police, they can be quickly labelled as the vulnerable *'victim'*. This terminology can be instantly disempowering for the person who is reporting the crime and could easily weaken their resolve.

Sadly, it is often the case that when survivors do muster the necessary courage to report domestic abuse and stalking behaviour, they are not always believed. Due to system overload or management challenges within the police force, time pressures, lack of specific training or ignorance within the departments, the victim's full story is often not heard or recorded. Therefore, the full context or the pattern of the abuse that they have endured is not always obvious, truly recognised, or really understood.

Following the rape and murder of Sarah Everard by the serving Met Police Officer Wayne Cousins, people had a sudden distinct lack of confidence in the police.

The 'End Violence Against Women' coalition www.endviolenceagainstwomen.org reported in November 2021 that almost 46% of women and 40% of men had less trust in the police and over 70% of all adults in their poll thought that the culture of policing had to change in response to violence against women and girls. To help regain public trust, the (NPCC) National Police Chiefs Council launched a new framework on 15 December 2021, which set out the action required from every police force in England and Wales to deliver a fundamental shift in priority of (VAWG) Violence Against Women and Girls to make it safer for them and to provide victims with a consistently high standard of service wherever they are.

The Victims' Commissioner for England and Wales, Dame Vera Baird QC, stated: *"If we are to effectively tackle violence against women and girls then we need to see a fundamental shift in culture within policing. The police need to relentlessly target and pursue offenders, but they also need to consistently challenge their own officers' sexist and misogynistic behaviours where they occur. The police approach to tackling VAWG won't change unless it challenges and changes itself."*

https://news.npcc.police.uk/releases/violent-men-who-harm-women-warned-that-police-are-increasing-action-against-them

Cruelty Towards Pets

Stalkers and perpetrators of domestic violence may kill, threaten to kill, or deliberately harm pet animals to exert dominance and power over their victims and these tactics are used to show them what could perhaps happen to them. Animal abuse is also often used as an attempt to silence or scare victims and is a significant barrier that prevents them from leaving violent relationships.

Filing false theft charges against the victim if they do leave the relationship with their pet is also common, and this is sometimes actioned by the perpetrator to deliberately cause extreme heartache for the victim, who then will experience further trauma and additional expense through fighting legal pet custody battles.

The perpetrator may also mistreat or give the pet away to exploit the emotional bond between the victim and the companion animal. Having experienced this first-hand myself, I struggle to find the right words to describe the devasting effect that this had and continues to have on me.

The National Link Coalition have recognised that mistreating animals is no longer seen as an isolated incident that can be ignored as it is often an indicator or predictor of crime and a 'red flag' warning sign that other family members in the household may not be safe. The mission of the National Link Coalition is to promote and maintain the only international resource centre addressing the link between animal cruelty and human violence to promote access to these services worldwide.

The National Link Coalition is working to prevent animal cruelty, domestic violence, child maltreatment and elder abuse by showing how they intersect. They recognise that when animals are abused, people are at risk and when people are abused, animals are at risk. Further information can be found on their website:

https://nationallinkcoalition.org

The "Power and Control Wheel" of Animal Abuse and Domestic Violence

Isolation: Refusing to allow the victim to take their pet to the vet or prohibiting them from socializing the animal.

Threats: To harm or kill the pet(s) if they leave or assert independence.

Denying & Blaming: Blaming the victim or pet for the perpetrators cruelty. Harming the pet and saying it was for the pets own good.

Legal Abuse: Custody battle over pets. Filing theft charges when they leave with the pets.

Emotional Abuse: Giving away or harming pets to exploit the emotional bond between the victim and the companion animal.

Economic Abuse: Refusing to allow the victim to spend money on pet food or vet care.

Intimidation: Harming or killing the pet and saying "Next time it'll be you". Targeting pets of family/friends who aid the victim in leaving.

Using children: Harming/killing pets to intimidate them. Blaming the disappearance of the family pet on the victim to create tension between them.

VIOLENCE

Isolation — Emotional Abuse
Threats — Economic Abuse
Denying & Blaming — Intimidation
Legal Abuse — Using Children

POWER AND CONTROL

Preparing Yourself for the Courtroom

If the Crown Prosecution Service (CPS) decide to support your case with the police and make the decision to prosecute the perpetrator, it is vitally important to prepare yourself emotionally and practically for attending the court to testify.

In the words of the Secret Barrister in **'Stories of the Law and How It's Broken'** *"Entering the criminal justice system as a victim will test your patience, often to destruction and beyond repair as you stumble into a vortex of poor performance, delays and inefficiencies."* (The Secret Barrister, 2018, p138).

This may be the very first time you have ever entered a court building. In which case, you will be given information about the process of court proceedings. You will also be offered a chance to visit the court building and enter the courtroom with a clerk to familiarise yourself with the surroundings prior to your court case. You will be able to stand at the lectern where you may have to stand on the day of the trial to give evidence. This prior knowledge and first-hand experience will really help to reduce your fears. Make sure that you take full advantage of all the support and advice that is freely available. Ask as many questions as you can to reassure yourself about the process. This will give you the necessary knowledge and confidence to ultimately fight for the justice that you deserve. You do not have to face your perpetrator if you choose not to as a screen can be provided, or in some cases, you can attend court proceedings via a video link.

Your presence in court, and your written and spoken words, are the first keys to a successful outcome, particularly if your case is taking place in the Crown Court with a jury. However, being physically present in the courtroom and hearing the voice of the perpetrator, who may indeed deny or lie about the events that have happened can be very traumatic. It is important to be prepared to hear facts being disclosed about you within the courtroom, which may indeed be incorrect or be deliberately misconstrued by the defence team to your detriment.

Court procedures can be frustrating for the victim, as their voice is not always fully heard. If the perpetrator has a good defence barrister acting for them, victims will often have to experience listening to some very unfair comments and legal decisions.

If your perpetrator was manipulative and deceitful during your relationship, then expect them to continue to repeat that same behaviour. Now that they are being challenged by the legal system, they will probably be very antagonistic, and more intent on destroying your reputation if they can.

Expect the planned dates for attendance in court to be delayed, changed or cancelled at the last minute. This tends to happen often. If the perpetrator suddenly changes their plea from *'not guilty'* to *'guilty'*, then the court case may not even go ahead as planned. In such cases, a more lenient and lighter sentence may be issued by the Judge in recognition of the perpetrator's decision to change a plea to *'guilty'*. This is because, ultimately, this will save on court costs and court time. When the perpetrator opts for a plea bargain, this can be very distressing for the victim who has possibly been waiting for months, or even years, preparing for the court process and is keen to eventually have their day in court to be finally heard and to witness justice being done.

It is frustrating and it feels extremely unfair that the perpetrator seems to have more assistance and control over the legal procedure. They are allowed to liaise with their defence lawyer regularly, and they have full access to all the evidence against them. The victim, in comparison, has limited access to information during Crown Court proceedings, as the CPS solicitor and the prosecuting barrister are immediately in charge of events once the indictment becomes *'Regina v Perpetrator x'*. Immediately the victim is then known as the *'complainant'* and is very much on the periphery during the whole process. A victim is not personally represented by a barrister and therefore will have limited access to any information regarding pre-trial proceedings or the trial until after giving evidence.

Hearings at the Crown Court and Civil Court are nearly always recorded, so, if for any reason you are unable to attend a court hearing regarding your case, you can make a written request for a full transcript of the case from the court by applying online: https://www.gov.uk/apply-transcript-court-tribunal-hearing. This application may require authorisation from the presiding Judge who dealt with your specific case, and in most cases, the victim will have to pay for the full cost of this service. Be prepared to wait for some time, maybe weeks for the transcript to be forwarded to you. Alternatively, or in addition, you can always ask a friend to attend court on your behalf to observe the proceedings from the public gallery, if the proceedings are not closed to the public.

It is very difficult for the victim to keep faith, stay strong and fight for their rights at a time when they are feeling particularly weak and vulnerable. Inevitably, they must recognise and accept that the decision regarding the sentencing for the crime which has been committed against them, will ultimately rest with the professional performance of the acting barristers on the day, the Jury, (if in the Crown Court), and ultimately, the Judge.

In the book: *The Secret Barrister – Stories of the Law and How it is Broken* (Macmillan, 2018), a worthwhile read for anyone experiencing the court process for the first time, the author states in no uncertain terms that: *'The trial process and court's judgement can tear a life apart'* (2018, p8). It is also important to be fully aware that *'...defendants, victims and, ultimately, society are being failed daily by an entrenched disregard for fundamental principles of fairness'*, (2018, p9).

Assessing the Possible Danger to Life

Dr Jane Monkton Smith, a former police officer and a forensic criminologist who specialises in domestic homicide, coercive control, and stalking, conducted a study in 2018 of women who were killed by their male partners. After investigating all the cases on the **'Counting Dead Women'** website **(1)**, she discovered that in 372 of the killings, almost all of them followed an eight-step pattern. There were several cases of male victims who were killed by their male partners. However, Dr Jane Monkton Smith states that women account for more than 80% of victims who were killed by their partners, and most of the time the partner is male.

My daughter had observed the escalating psychological abuse that I was experiencing from my partner, and she was becoming increasingly concerned for my well-being. She emailed me a copy of Dr Jane Monkton Smith's **'Eight Stage Intimate Partner Homicide Timeline' (2)**. I will never forget her saying to me, *'Mum, please read these 8 stages – you are at stage 7 now, and stage 8 is homicide.'*

It was my daughter's courage and her support and tenacity that saved my life. She was terrified to discover that the pattern of abuse that I was experiencing was identical to the 8 stages of the 'Homicide Timeline', so she contacted the local police to request an application to **'Clare's Law'** on my behalf, to find out if my partner had a criminal history of abuse. The police quickly responded to her request and asked where I was. Although they could not disclose any details about my partner's criminal history to her, they did confirm that my life could be in danger. Following receipt of this information and with the help of police, lawyers, family and friends, I did manage to plan an escape from my partner's abusive, coercive, and controlling behaviour. Fortunately, I survived his violent attack, and I was able to get the necessary support that I required.

Anyone in a relationship who has valid concerns about their partner's history can apply via **'Clare's Law'** for a disclosure of any previous convictions of domestic violence. This is known as the **'DVDS' – Domestic Violence Disclosure Scheme (3)**. A close relative can also apply via the police for the disclosure on behalf of the concerned person, although it must be noted that any detailed information regarding previous offences will only be shared directly with the person who is the intimate partner within the relationship. These facts are normally disclosed in a face-to-face meeting with the victim, and any information is provided verbally and is not given out in any written form. The person will have to contractually agree not to publicly share the information that has been given to them regarding this disclosure.

I can highly recommend to anyone who has real concerns about their partner's behaviour towards them, to make an application via the police to **'Clare's Law'**. The process is simple, and having access to this knowledge is a very empowering tool. The information will aid recognition of any possible risks and provide the necessary self-confidence and motivation to create a clear safety plan. If required, the applicant will be given full access to local services and any vital support if they wish to devise an escape route from a potentially dangerous situation.

Fortunately, I can now say that I am a survivor. However, it has been a long, traumatic and torturous journey to eventually be able to achieve a satisfactory outcome where I can begin to feel safe. For over two years,

I was living in fear for my life and in a constant hyper-vigilant state, hiding out in various secret locations to escape my partner's persistent fixated abusive behaviour and stalking. This experience has inevitably had a drastic and devastating effect on my physical and mental well-being.

I experienced the harrowing process of preparing numerous detailed statements to defend myself against the fictitious charges that my partner deliberately instigated against me. These charges resulted in complex and expensive court cases. His actions appeared to be a deliberate and malicious attempt by him to cause me further harm and distress. I spent hours each day collating the required evidence and writing the documents that were required by the lawyers and the police to prepare for the court cases, but it was worth doing this work myself to eventually achieve justice.

(1) *Counting Dead Women* –
https://kareningalasmith.com/counting-dead-women

(2) *In Control – Dangerous relationships and how they end in murder* (Jane Monckton Smith, 2021)

(3) Clare's Law/Domestic Violence Disclosure Scheme (DVDS):
www.gov.uk/government/publications/domestic-abuse-bill-2020-factsheets/domestic-violence-disclosure-scheme-factsheet

Keeping Safe

If the perpetrator receives a prison sentence, the victim may naively consider that justice has been done and they may begin to relax and think that they can feel free and safe again. However, in most cases, the guilty party will only serve half the sentence period that has been given to them, and then they will be released on probation. Often this means that following their early release from prison, they may choose to live near the victim. This can be a terrifying thought for the victim, particularly if no restraining order or stalking protection order has been put in place.

The release of the perpetrator from prison is recognised as an extremely dangerous time for the victim, particularly if the perpetrator has a violent nature or has been convicted of stalking. Often the perpetrators who have just been released from prison are feeling extremely bitter and angry, and they may aim to seek revenge.

Due to Human Rights Law, on release from prison, any information regarding the address or location of the perpetrator cannot be disclosed to the victim. However, unfortunately, in most cases, the perpetrator will know exactly where to find the victim. Therefore, it is imperative that the victim shares any of their personal safety concerns with the police and their allocated **Independent Domestic Violence Advisor (IDVA),** and/or the probation team, (if this is appropriate), to ensure that the correct safety measures are put in place. Initiating a thorough safety plan, being vigilant, and having regular contact with the police and the probation team will be essential for the safety of the victim at this time.

The probation service works to protect the public and to reduce reoffending. However, a specialist area of probation work is also to provide victim support. Currently, a victim of a serious offence who is concerned about their personal safety may be able to request or be offered the opportunity to engage with a **Victim Liaison Officer (VLO)** from the probation service. The allocated Victim Liaison Officer will assist them in establishing a voice within the justice system and will provide the victim with the necessary details about the criminal justice system. They will also assist with establishing the necessary exclusion zones for the offender when released from custody, and keep the victim updated on any sentencing developments. This can be very empowering and reassuring for the victim.

It may also be necessary to apply for a **Stalking Protection Order (SPO)**, or a **Restraining Order,** (if this is not already arranged). If this is in place, the police can then offer the necessary immediate action or support for the victim if it is required. Sometimes, these measures are automatically initiated or endorsed by the Judge when sentencing takes place, but this is not always the case. Each case is considered on its own merit and therefore, these orders can vary considerably in content from the list of actions that the perpetrator is prevented from doing to the places where the perpetrator is excluded from, and the number of months/years that the order is valid for.

In high-risk scenarios, most victims will appeal for a life-long restraining order to be put in place, but sadly it is rare that a Judge will issue these. It is something that many victims cannot comprehend. What difference does it make to a Judge whether the order is fixed for two years, five years, ten years or life-long? Nothing. However, to a traumatised victim of stalking, and/or domestic abuse this could make the difference between life and death.

With the increasing availability of inexpensive but sophisticated surveillance equipment and other devices, it is very easy for stalkers and abusers to track down and terrorise their prey. This is often referred to as **'cyberstalking'**. The popular everyday use of mobile phones and social media accounts provides numerous opportunities for victims to be easily traced and monitored by the perpetrator. Therefore, it is important to make sure that any passwords and protection modes to prevent public access are regularly checked, changed and/or updated on social media accounts.

On a more positive note, several charities have designed various apps for phones that can be used to signal for urgent help or support if needed. The police can also provide the most vulnerable victims with an emergency app on their phone which will show their location if used and will provide immediate police assistance when necessary. Again, the onus is often on the victim to make a request for such items.

Vicarious Trauma

Often family members, friends, or children of victims who are being stalked and/or abused by their partners will vicariously experience psychological trauma by either unwillingly observing such behaviour happening, hearing about it from others, or by being directly involved.

Vicarious trauma needs to be more widely recognized and understood as it can have devastating life-changing effects on those who experience it. Relatives or people closely associated to victims who are murdered by their abusive partners, or a stalker can find it extremely hard to come to terms with what has happened. They may blame themselves for not noticing the significant signs that have led to this happening, or indeed, feel guilty and remorseful for not acting sooner after witnessing the behaviour that they had observed. Relatives and friends can struggle for years trying to come to terms with what has happened, and they may be forever plagued by regret, wondering for the rest of their lives if the outcome might have been different if they had spoken out earlier.

Sometimes relatives may have strong suspicions that domestic abuse is happening to someone within the family, but they might feel unsure whether they should intervene. They may not have the necessary knowledge or confidence to offer guidance or support to help. However, I hope the information in my book may change this view, and that those onlookers who suspect domestic abuse will be more proactive in voicing their concerns and will make a conscious effort to assist victims in finding the correct help and support that they require to be able to escape their dangerous situation.

If the victim is experiencing coercive control, violent physical abuse, and gas-lighting behaviour from the perpetrator they will understandably be extremely fearful of the consequences if they do decide to share what is happening to them with their family or friends. Victims of domestic violence will often lie about what is really happening to them to cover up their partner's behaviour, as they are afraid that disclosing such information may anger the perpetrator and instigate the possibility of further violent abuse which could endanger their life.

It is important to be aware that perpetrators of such violence will sometimes deliberately manipulate the situation by using devious ways, (for example, creating false stories to cast the victim in a bad light), with the sole intention of humiliating, intimidating, harming, punishing, and more worryingly isolating their partner from any opportunities to communicate with family of friends. The perpetrator's main objective is to damage any existing close relationships knowing that this will leave the victim in a more vulnerable position where they will no longer have anyone who they can turn to for help.

On 4th February 2023, Emma Pattison, the head of Epson College was shot and killed by her husband along with her seven-year-old daughter Lettie after which George Pattison shot himself with a sporting shotgun. Emma's sister Deborah Kirk wrote a touching tribute to her sister for the Sunday Times Magazine which was published on Sunday 10th December 2023 in which she writes with such clarity and wisdom about when the police informed her about how her sister and her niece had suffered not only on the night that they were killed, but also prior to this how they had been exposed to a pattern of domestic abuse.

Deborah shares how she has embraced therapy to assist her to deal with her overwhelming grief and utter regret that she did not spot the real danger that her sister was in. Deborah found that writing poetry and songs have helped her to move forwards to begin accepting such loss. (*'Letters to my sister'* Kirk, Deborah, 2023. Article in The Sunday Times Magazine, 10 December 2023).
https://www.thetimes.co.uk/article/my-sister-was-killed-at-epsom-college-these-are-my-letters-to-her-xl3q3nwb0

Recovering From Trauma and Fear

The victims and survivors of abuse who shared their stories for this book are still struggling to come to terms with what has happened to them. Reflecting on their own experiences, some of them are now actively championing a change to the laws that exist in the UK regarding stalking and domestic abuse. Others have found new and rewarding employment in organisations that support victims of abuse and one survivor has written a book.

Psychological fear is in our minds and stalkers and abusers are fully aware of this. In their mission to assert power and control over their victim, they will deliberately take advantage of using certain known facts and tactics to continue to harass and mentally disturb the victim for possibly years after the conviction. Therefore, it is vitally important to speak out and share your story and your concerns with others, be it family, friends or a professional organisation.

Conquering a way through the experience of such traumatic events, and being able to find the energy, and self-efficacy to commence a new path forward in life is challenging but as shown by the survivors that I have met during the writing of this book, they demonstrate that it is entirely possible. The knowledge and support of others who have had similar experiences of stalking and abuse will often provide the necessary momentum to build up the courage, strength, and resilience to triumph over adversity.

'I learned that courage was not the absence of fear, but the triumph over it. The brave man is not he who does not feel afraid but he who conquers that fear.'

Nelson Mandela

The 8-Stage Homicide Timeline

If you are suffering abuse in your relationship or know someone who is, do not ignore the valuable research by Dr Jane Monckton Smith as it may help to assess the risk or threat to your life. Each of these eight stages is explained in more detail in the book: *'In Control – Dangerous relationships and how they end in murder'* (Jane Monckton Smith, 2021).

The only instance where a stage in the timeline was not followed was when the perpetrator did not meet stage one. However, this was normally because the perpetrator had not been in a relationship before.

The 8-Stage Homicide Timeline
(Jane Monckton Smith, 2021)

1. A pre-relationship **history of stalking or abuse** by the perpetrator.

2. The romance **developing quickly** into a serious relationship.

3. The relationship becoming dominated by **coercive control**.

4. A **trigger** to threaten the perpetrator's control – for example, the relationship ends or the perpetrator gets into financial difficulty.

5. **Escalation** – an increase in the intensity or frequency of the partner's control tactics, such as stalking or threatening suicide.

6. The perpetrator has a **change in thinking** – choosing to move on, either through revenge or by homicide.

7. **Planning** – the perpetrator might buy weapons or seek opportunities to get the victim alone.

8. **Homicide** – The perpetrator kills his or her partner and possibly hurts others such as the victim's children.

**Do not ignore these patterns of abuse.
Watch out and speak out.**

Watch Out

When you feel uneasy
Listen to your instinct
Watch out!

When he moves on you too quickly
And says you are the only love of his life
Watch out!

When he has glaring eyes
But smiles with his mouth
Watch out!

When he has a nervous tic
And fiddles with his hands
Watch out!

When you discover he is lying
About events that have occurred
Watch out!

When he creates fictitious stories
About his neurotic ex-partner
Watch out!

When he makes you feel sorry for him
And plays on you with the tears
Watch out!

When he is very needy
And he bombards you with his calls
Watch out!

When he criticises your family
And distances you from your friends
Watch out!

When he demands your attention
Every moment of the day
Watch out!

When he behaves like a spoilt child
With temper tantrums and sulks
Watch out!

When he spies on you and lurks around
And violates you
Get out!

Melissa Stockdale
(2021)

Acknowledgements

I would like to thank the wonderful staff at **'Lighthouse Women's Aid'** for listening, believing and validating my own personal experiences of domestic abuse. They were non-judgemental and they responded to me with compassion and professional integrity. The *'Freedom Program'* that they offered was educational and empowering. It was their early caring input that enabled me to make positive decisions about my future, assisted my emotional recovery, and their belief in me that motivated me to write this book.

I would also like to express my gratitude to my two loving children and my faithful friends who stood by me throughout my ordeal, and to all the wonderful professional people who supported and encouraged me through those challenging and fearful years of stalking and abuse from 2019 to 2022.

Many thanks to Keith Abbott and Karolina Robinson Zammit at MTP Agency for patiently working with me to produce this book.

List of Helpful Information

I sincerely hope that the publication of this book will assist those who are caught up in abusive relationships and that it will provide them with the vital information, necessary tools and the confidence to seek help. Traumatised and fearful survivors, who are brave enough to take that first step to report the crime against them, deserve to be treated with dignity and respect.

Alice Ruggles Trust: https://alicerugglestrust.org

Applications for Court Transcripts:
https://www.gov.uk/apply-transcript-court-tribunal-hearing

'Ask For ANI' (Action Needed Immediately) – **UK SAYS NO MORE**: A national campaign to raise awareness of abuse and sexual violence. Over 6000 locations are now registered as 'safe places' to report sexual and domestic violence and abuse, including Boots, Superdrug and Morrison's stores:
https://uksaysnomore.org/get-involved/ask-for-ani/

Clare's Law/Domestic Violence Disclosure Scheme (DVDS):
www.gov.uk/government/publications/domestic-abuse-bill-2020-factsheets/domestic-violence-disclosure-scheme-factsheet

Counting Dead Women:
https://kareningalasmith.com/counting-dead-women

Hollie Gazzard Trust: https://holliegazzard.org

How to Guide: Words & Pictures:
https://www.cescp.org.uk/pdf/signs-of-safety/how-to-guide-words-and-pictures.pdf

Leeway Domestic Violence and Abuse Services:
https://www.leewaysupport.org
Domestic Abuse Helpline: 0300 561 0077

Men's Advice Line: Helpline: 0808 2000 247

The National Link Coalition:
https://nationallinkcoalition.org

The National Stalking Helpline: 0808 802 0300
Email: advice@stalkinghelpline.org

The Network for Surviving Stalking (NSS):
www.scaredofsomeone.org is the leading charity in the United Kingdom dedicated to supporting victims of stalking.

Stalking Risk Profile:
www.stalkingriskprofile.com/victim-support/victim-resource-links

Paladin National Stalking Advocacy Service:
0203 866 4107 www.paladinservice.co.uk is a charity that trains Independent Stalking Advocacy Caseworkers (ISACs) to assist high-risk victims of stalking in England and Wales.

Protection Against Stalking:
www.protectionagainststalking.org

Rights of Women: **Children and the law**: **the Family Court process**: https://rightsofwomen.org.uk

Safelives – Ending domestic abuse:
https://safelives.org.uk

SAMM National – Support After Murder and Manslaughter: https://samm.org.uk
0121 472 2912 Text: 07342 888570

Section 76 of The Serious Crime Act 2015:
https://www.legislation.gov.uk/ukpga/2015/9/section/7
6/enatcted

Sexual Assault Referral Centre (SARC):
https://www.nhs.uk/service-search/other-services/Rape-and-sexual-assault-referral-centres/LocationSearch/36

The Suzy Lamplugh Trust: 020 7091 0014 Email:
info@suzylamplugh.org
www.suzylamplugh.org

Victim's Commissioner:
https://victimscommissioner.org.uk

The Victim Personal Statement:
https://www.cps.gov.uk/sites/default/files/documents/le
gal_guidance/joint-agency-guide-victim-personal-statement_0.pdf

Victim Support: 0845 3030 900
www.victimsupport.org.uk

Victim Support for stalking:
https://www.victimsupport.org.uk/stalking/support

Women's Aid: Helpline 0808 2000 247
www.womensaid.org.uk

Refuge National Domestic Abuse Helpline
www.nationalhelpline.org.uk

Bibliography

Bulstrode, M. (2007, February 24) East Anglian Daily Times, p.2.

BBC News (2022, November 25) Stalking Super - complaint launched against police. https://www.bbc.co.uk/news/uk-63745857

Day, E. (2013, February 17) The Stalking Cure. *The Guardian,* pp. 17-20.

Domestic Abuse Act 2021 https://www.legislation.gov.uk/ukpga/2021/17section/23

End Violence Against Women coalition https://www.endviolenceagainstwomen.org

Gaddis, W. (1994) *A Frolic of His Own.*

Hadjimatheou, K. (2022) *'Social care told me I had to': Empowerment and responsibilisation in the Domestic Violence Disclosure Scheme.'- The British Journal of Criminology, 62 (2). pp. 320-336. ISSN 0007-0955*

Hare, Robert D, (1993) *Without Conscience – The disturbing world of the psychopaths among us.*

Ingala Smith, K. (2022) *Counting Dead Women* -
https://kareningalasmith.com/counting-dead-women

Kirk, D. (2023) *'Letters to my sister'* Article in The Sunday
Times Magazine, 10 December 2023).
https://www.thetimes.co.uk/article/my-sister-was-killed-
at-epsom-college-these-are-my-letters-to-her-xl3q3nwb0

Korkodeilou, J. (2020) *Victims of Stalking – Case Studies in
Invisible Harms.*

Kowalski, R. M. (Ed). (2001) *Behaving badly: Aversive
behaviours in interpersonal relationships.* Washington, DC:
American Psychological Association.

Leeway Domestic Violence and Abuse Services
https://www.leewaysupport.org

Mechanic, M., Weaver, T., & Resick, P. (2008). Mental
health consequences of intimate partner abuse: A
multidimensional assessment of form different forms of
abuse. *Violence Against Women, 14, 634-654.*

Monckton Smith, J. (2021) *In Control. Dangerous
relationships and how they end in murder.* Bloomsbury
Publishing.

National Police Chiefs Council (2021)
https://news.npcc.police.uk/releases/violent-men-who-
harm-women-warned-that-police-are-increasing-action-
against-them

Nuttall, D., (2007, February 23 - updated 2021, February 18) Family's anguish over killer's sentence. *East Anglian Daily Times>News*

Office for National Statistics (2022) Crime and Justice. https://www.ons.gov.uk>crimeandjustice

Paulhus, D., & Williams, Kevin M. (2002) *The Dark Triad of Personality: Narcissism, Machiavellianism, and Psychopathy.* Journal of Research in Personality 36(6): 556-563.

The Secret Barrister. (2018) *Stories of the Law and How it's Broken.* Macmillan.

When it's
a pattern,
it's abuse.

When it's
a pattern,
it's abuse.

Where are you? Who are you with? I don't like her. That friend is horrible. Don't you think you should go out less? Maybe you should stay in tonight? I don't want you going out anymore. Remember, I'm watching you.

Coercive control
is repeated behaviour
designed to control,
manipulate or frighten.
It's against the law.

Donate £10 to support women
experiencing domestic abuse.
www.womensaid.org.uk

women's aid
until women & children are safe

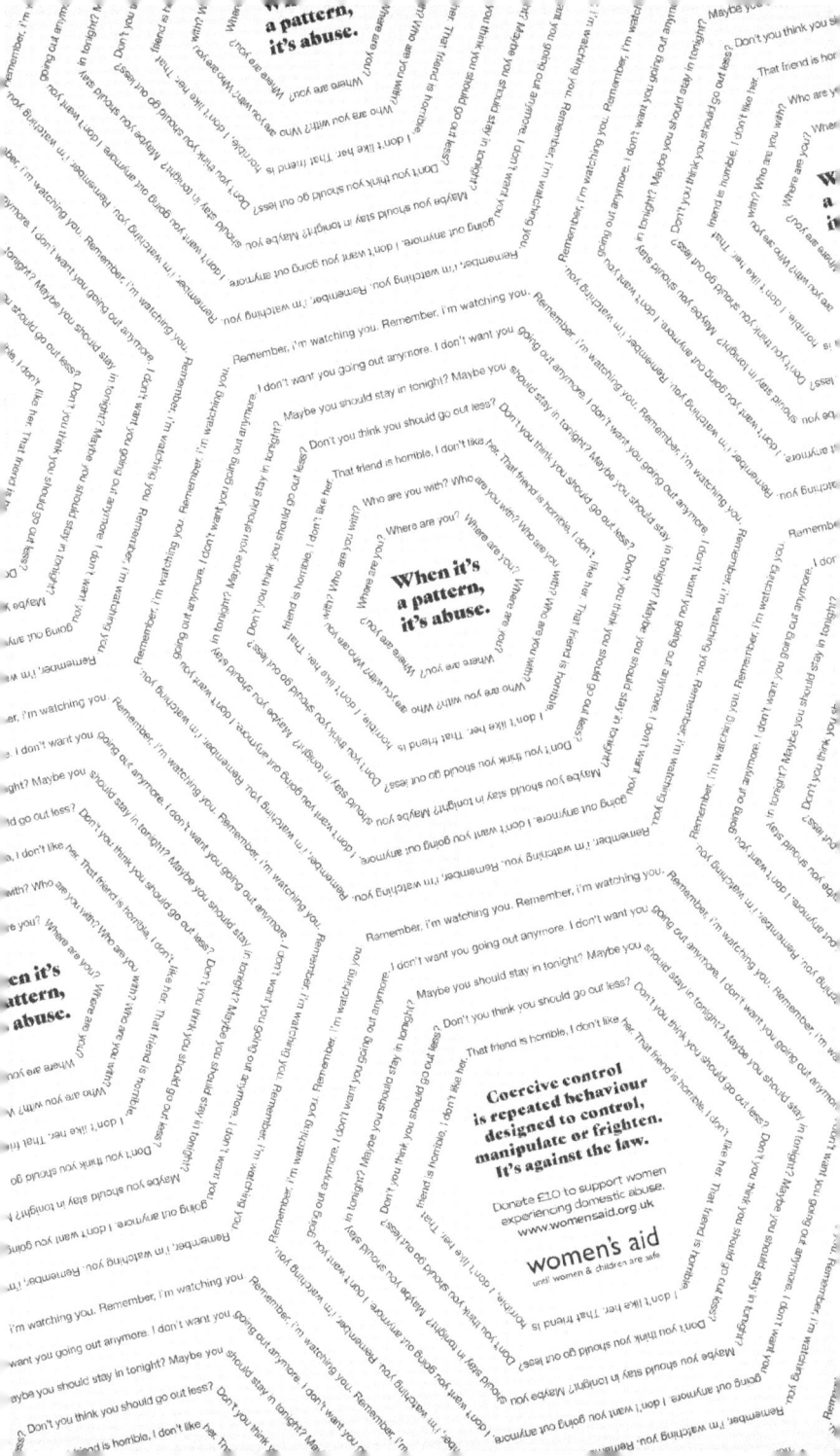

Available worldwide from Amazon
and all good bookstores

———————————

Michael Terence
Publishing

www.mtp.agency

www.facebook.com/mtp.agency

@mtp_agency

www.ingramcontent.com/pod-product-compliance
Ingram Content Group UK Ltd.
Pitfield, Milton Keynes, MK11 3LW, UK
UKHW031315170225
4629UKWH00035B/376